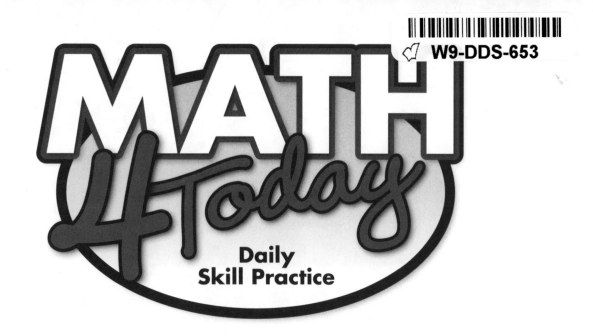

Grade 4

Carson-Dellosa Publishing LLC
Greensboro, North Carolina

Credits
Content Editor: Bitsy Griffin
Copy Editor: Elise Craver

Visit *carsondellosa.com* for correlations to Common Core, state, national, and Canadian provincial standards.

Carson-Dellosa Publishing LLC
PO Box 35665
Greensboro, NC 27425 USA
carsondellosa.com

ISBN 978-1-4838-4163-2
03-161191151

Table of Contents

Introduction

Math 4 Today: Daily Skill Practice is a comprehensive yet quick and easy-to-use supplement to any classroom math curriculum. This series will strengthen students' math skills as they review numbers, operations, algebraic thinking, measurement, data, and geometry.

This book covers 40 weeks of daily practice. Essential math skills are reviewed each day during a four-day period with an assessment of the skills practiced on the fifth day. Each week includes a math fluency practice section, intended to be a quick one-minute activity that encourages fluency in math facts. For more detailed fluency tips, see pages 5 and 6. The week concludes with a math journal prompt.

Various skills and concepts are reinforced throughout the book through activities that align to the state standards. To view these standards, see the Standards Alignment Chart on page 7.

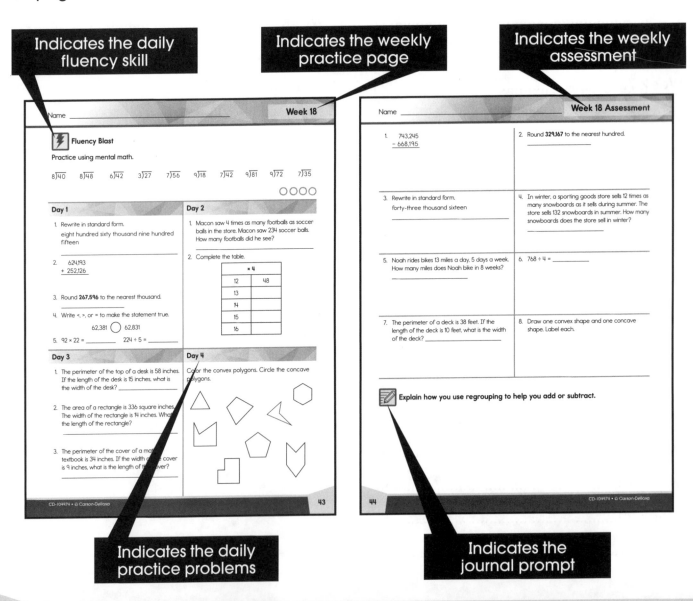

Indicates the daily fluency skill

Indicates the weekly practice page

Indicates the weekly assessment

Indicates the daily practice problems

Indicates the journal prompt

Developing Fluency

One of the primary goals of every teacher is to help students learn basic math facts accurately, recall them fluently, and retain that fluency over time. Fluency is the stage of learning where the learner acquires the information at an automatic level. A student must have this fluency of math facts in order to perform multi-digit algorithms and problem solve efficiently.

Math strategies should be introduced and reinforced daily to develop number sense. Opportunity is lost to develop number sense when math facts are taught only through rote memorization. The key to using strategies for basic facts is to have students discover the patterns in addition and multiplication and name them. For example, in addition, students may recognize doubles facts. In multiplication, students may see that 1 times any number equals the same number.

The ability to effortlessly recall math facts lessens students' anxiety and increases their confidence when engaging in more challenging math tasks.

Math Fluency Activities

Use these fun and easy games to engage students in practicing math facts.
- **Dice Roll**—Roll two dice. Use the numbers to practice adding, subtracting, multiplying, dividing, and creating fractions.
- **Flash Card Swat**—Using flash cards, students flip over two cards at a time. Students should use a flyswatter to swat a card they think they know the answer to and say the answer.
- **Race the Room**—Tape a long piece of bulletin board paper to a wall. Have teams of students stand on the opposite side of the room. Say math facts and have students race to the paper and write the answers.
- **War**—Using a deck of cards, students flip over two cards and add (or multiply). Whoever says the correct sum (or product) first keeps the cards.

Using the Fluency Blast

The fluency blast section is designed for students to use mental math on a daily basis. It is not intended that students write the answers each day. Students should practice the fluency blast facts for the week every day (excluding assessment day). Have students color a bubble for each day of practice. Begin the activity by setting a timer for one minute (or 30 seconds). To ensure students are practicing the math facts accurately, post an answer key on the first day.

Tracking Fluency

Have students use the reproducible on page 6 to track their progress. First, students should set a time for when they would like to meet their fluency goals. Then, they should fill in the blank spaces with the math facts they would like to practice. Finally, have students color a section as they master each goal. This page can be used monthly, quarterly, or throughout the entire school year.

Name _____

Fact Fluency Blastoff!

My goal is to know all of my _____ facts

by _____.

Fact

Fact

Fact

Fact

Fact

Fact

Fact

Fact

Fact

Fact

**I know
all of my
_____
facts!**

Standards Alignment Chart

State Standards*		Weeks
Operations and Algebraic Thinking		
Use the four operations with whole numbers to solve problems.	4.OA.1–4.OA.3	1–40
Gain familiarity with factors and multiples.	4.OA.4	3–10, 13, 15, 17, 23, 26
Generate and analyze patterns.	4.OA.5	1–12, 14–21, 28–30, 33–35, 37, 39
Number and Operations in Base Ten		
Generalize place value understanding for multi-digit whole numbers.	4.NBT.1–4.NBT.3	1–13, 15–22, 25, 29, 31–35, 37, 39
Use place value understanding and properties of operations to perform multi-digit arithmetic.	4.NBT.4–4.NBT.6	1–20, 24, 30–32, 34, 36, 38
Number and Operations—Fractions		
Extend understanding of fraction equivalence and ordering.	4.NF.1–4.NF.2	6, 7, 21–40
Build fractions from unit fractions.	4.NF.3–4.NF.4	21–40
Understand decimal notation for fractions, and compare decimal fractions.	4.NF.5–4.NF.7	21, 24–29, 31, 32, 38–40
Measurement and Data		
Solve problems involving measurement and conversion of measurement.	4.MD.1–4.MD.3	1–20
Represent and interpret data.	4.MD.4	1, 21–29
Geometric measurement: understand concept of angle and measure angles.	4.MD.5–4.MD.7	30–40
Geometry		
Draw and identify lines and angles, and classify shapes by properties of their lines and angles.	4.G.1–4.G.3	1–40

The research is clear that family involvement is strongly linked to student success. Support for student learning at home improves student achievement in school. Educators should not underestimate the significance of this connection.

The fluency activities in this book create an opportunity to create or improve this school-to-home link. Students are encouraged to practice their math fluency facts at home with their families each week. Parents and guardians can use the reproducible tracking sheet (below) to record how their students performed in their fluency practice during the week. Students should be encouraged to return the tracking sheet to the teacher at the end of the week.

In order to make the school-to-home program work for students and their families, it may be helpful to reach out to them with an introductory letter. Explain the program and its intent and ask them to partner with you in their children's educational process. Describe the role you expect them to play. Encourage them to offer suggestions or feedback along the way.

Name _____ Week of_____

Fact Fluency: Practice Makes Perfect!

Day	Fact(s) I practiced	How I practiced	How I feel about these facts
M		☐ flash cards ☐ worksheet ☐ game ☐ other _____	☺ ☐ ☹
T		☐ flash cards ☐ worksheet ☐ game ☐ other _____	☺ ☐ ☹
W		☐ flash cards ☐ worksheet ☐ game ☐ other _____	☺ ☐ ☹
Th		☐ flash cards ☐ worksheet ☐ game ☐ other _____	☺ ☐ ☹

Fluency Blast

Practice using mental math.

15	51	44	13	28	29	64	88	49	11	25	33
+ 4	+ 6	+ 4	+ 6	+ 6	+ 3	+ 3	+ 4	+ 2	+ 5	+ 4	+ 6

○○○○

Day 1

1. 707
    − 59

2. 2,132
    + 59

3. Rewrite in standard form.

    one hundred thousand eighty-seven

    _____

4. Round each number to the nearest hundred.

    324 _____   458 _____

    656 _____   772 _____

Day 2

1. Sabena and Forrest were playing video games. Sabena scored 21,956 points and Forrest scored 9,077 points. How many points did Sabena and Forrest score altogether?

    _____

2. Complete the table.

×2	
5	10
10	
15	
20	
25	

Day 3

1. Write the time shown.

    _____

2. How many more students voted for baseball and basketball than football?

    _____

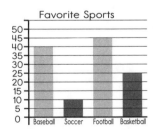

Favorite Sports

3. 360 in. = _____ yd.

Day 4

Name the line, ray, or angle.

1. M   N
    ●————————●——→   _____

2. X   Y
    ←——●————————●——→   _____

3. Color the triangles.

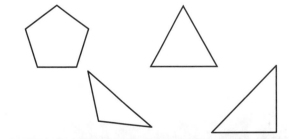

---

1. Round each number to the nearest hundred.

   481 _____

   221 _____

   152 _____

2. 33,976
   − 29,908
   _____

3. Rewrite in standard form.

   fifty-nine thousand six

   _____

4. Complete the table.

×3	
3	9
6	
9	
12	
15	

5. A fund-raiser for The Children's Museum raised $44,209. The museum spent $9,785 on food and beverages. How much money did the museum raise after paying for food and beverages? _____

6. Write the missing numbers to complete the pattern.

   10, 12, 14, _____, _____, _____

7. 10 ft. = _____ in.

8. Name the angle.

_____

 Use words, drawings, or numbers to explain how you would determine if 6 is prime or composite.

Fluency Blast

Practice using mental math.

19	23	15	38	39	47	14	18	55	85	15	60
− 6	− 7	− 2	− 3	− 2	− 8	− 3	− 6	−40	− 6	− 4	− 3

○○○○

Day 1

1. 91 + 25 + 13 = _____

2. What is the value of 2 quarters, 5 dimes, and 6 pennies? _____

3. 49,117
   − 34,469

4. Round **54,578** to the nearest ten thousand.

   _____

5. Write <, >, or = to make the statement true.

   17,987 ◯ 17,877

Day 2

1. Complete the table.

+4	
1	5
3	
8	
16	
20	

2. Tomorrow, 569 people will want to buy tickets to a concert. Only 415 tickets are available. How many people will not get tickets?

   _____

Day 3

1. What unit would you use to measure the length of a wall?

   A. millimeter   B. centimeter   C. meter

2. Write the time shown.

   _____

3. 7 mi. = _____ yd.

4. 2,400 in. = _____ ft.

Day 4

Identify each set of lines as **parallel**, **perpendicular**, or **intersecting**.

1.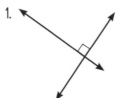

   _____

2.
   C   M

   L   S

   _____

   _____

3. D
   E
   F

   _____

1. Name the shape.

_____

2.   17,466
   − 7,756
   _____

3. Rewrite in standard form.

   60,000 + 5,000 + 300 + 5

   _____

4. Round **43,766** to the nearest thousand.

   _____

5. $1,358
   + $7,649
   _____

6. Complete the table.

+ 10	
41	51
57	
47	
52	
45	

7. Austin has to be at soccer practice by the time shown on the clock. What time does he have to be at soccer practice?

   _____

8. 3,000 ÷ 300 = _____

  Why do you think it is important to know how to write numbers in standard, expanded, and word forms?

Fluency Blast

Practice using mental math.

60	50	40	70	80	10	20	30	50	90	100	40
− 5	− 7	− 2	− 9	−10	− 1	−15	−18	−19	−12	− 16	−17

○○○○

Day 1

1. Write the multiplication sentence shown by the picture. _____

2. Rewrite in standard form.

   60,000 + 5,000 + 300 + 60 + 5 _____

3. Round each number to the nearest ten. Add.

   34 + 81 is about _____ .

4. List the factors of **8**. _____

   Is **8** prime or composite? _____

Day 2

1. Complete the table.

− 6	
125	119
126	
127	
128	
129	

2. Danielle is reading a book that is 587 pages long. She read 181 pages on Saturday and 205 pages on Sunday. She finished the book on Monday. How many pages did she read on Monday? _____

Day 3

1. 30 pt. = _____ qt.

2. 40 qt. = _____ gal.

3. 44 pt. = _____ c.

4. 20 c. = _____ oz.

5. 16 pt. = _____ qt.

Day 4

Identify each angle as **right**, **acute**, or **obtuse**.

1.

_____

2.

_____

3.

_____

1. Rewrite in standard form.

   50,000 + 5,000 + 400 + 60 + 3

   _____

2. Round **45,356** to the nearest hundred.

   _____

3. List the factors of **9**. _____

   Is **9** prime or composite? _____

4. Complete the table.

– 4	
500	496
525	
550	
575	
600	

5. Write the multiplication sentence shown by the picture. _____

6. Cory took 72 photos of animals at the zoo. He took 18 photos of monkeys, 23 of tigers, and 11 of polar bears. The remaining photos were of the elephants. How many photos did Cory take of the elephants? _____

7. 80 qt. = _____ pt.

8. 324 ft. = _____ yd.

 Explain how multiplying by 100 is different from multiplying by 10. How does understanding place value help you?

CD-104974 • © Carson-Dellosa

Fluency Blast

Practice using mental math.

$$\begin{array}{cccccccccccc} 2 & 5 & 8 & 4 & 9 & 8 & 0 & 3 & 6 & 1 & 10 & 7 \\ \times 6 & \times 2 & \times 8 & \times 9 & \times 3 & \times 1 & \times 8 & \times 3 & \times 4 & \times 10 & \times 5 & \times 7 \end{array}$$

○○○○○

Day 1

1. Rewrite in standard form.

   one million five hundred ninety-seven thousand seven hundred seventy-two

   _____

2. Round **182,983** to the nearest ten thousand.

   _____

3. 1,777
    +5,884

4. 2,239
    −2,182

Day 2

1. List the factors of **11.** _____

   Is **11** prime or composite? _____

2. Solve.

   30 × 2 _____

   30 × 3 _____

   30 × 4 _____

3. A tree branch has 7 buds. Each day, 3 more buds sprout. How many buds are on the tree branch after the first 5 days? (Hint: Draw a T-chart.) _____

Day 3

1. Complete the table.

m	cm
1	100
2	
3	
4	
5	

2. The zookeeper takes 300,000 milliliters of water to the elephants. How many liters of water does the zookeeper give the elephants?

   _____

Day 4

Identify each angle as **acute**, **right**, or **obtuse**.

1.

   _____

2.

   _____

3.

   _____

1. Heath earns $6 for each room he cleans in his house. If Heath cleans 2 rooms and buys a bag of candy for $3, how much money does he have left? _____

2.
$$\begin{array}{r} 1{,}237 \\ -954 \\ \hline \end{array}$$

3. $800 \div 8 =$ _____

4. Rewrite in standard form.

   7 ten thousands + 5 thousands + 3 hundreds + 1 ten + 7 ones

   _____

5. Round **81,298** to the nearest ten.

   _____

6. 100 m = _____ cm

7. The tree has 28 acorns under it. Each day, 3 more acorns fall under the tree. How many acorns are under the tree after the first 5 days? (Hint: Draw a T-chart.) _____

8. Identify the angle.

   _____

 Why is it helpful to use a T-chart for problem 7? What are some other situations in which using a T-chart would be helpful?

Fluency Blast

Practice using mental math.

2	1	4	8	5	4	2	6	9	3	6	0
× 3	× 7	× 4	× 6	× 7	× 0	× 9	× 5	× 6	× 8	×10	× 3

○○○○

Day 1

1. 900 ÷ 9 = _____

2. 66,869
    − 34,937

3. 43,273
    + 30,586

4. Round **867,433** to the nearest hundred thousand. _____

5. Write <, >, or = to make the statement true.

   15,898 ◯ 15,889

Day 2

1. Determine the 13th shape in the pattern.

   _____

2. India found 12 starfish. Each starfish has 5 arms. How many arms did the starfish have in all?

   _____

3. Solve for the missing factor.

   32 = 4 × _____   44 = 4 × _____

   24 = 4 × _____   40 = 4 × _____

4. Continue the multiples of 3.

   3, 6, 9, _____ , _____ , _____ ,

   _____ , _____

Day 3

1. 48 in. = _____ ft.

2. 3 mi. = _____ yd.

3. 24 qt. = _____ gal.

4. 18 c. = _____ pt.

5. 96 in. = _____ ft.

Day 4

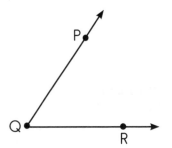

Name the geometric features.

1. rays: _____   _____

2. vertex: _____

3. angle: _____

Name _____

1. 6,000 ÷ 600 = _____

2. 2,626 + 7,625 = _____

3. 9,379 – 7,312 = _____

4. Determine the 18th shape in the pattern.

_____

5. Round **87,258** to the nearest thousand.

_____

6. Solve.

9 × 5 = _____

9 × 7 = _____

9 × 4 = _____

7. 720 yd. = _____ ft.

8. Rewrite in standard form.

one hundred ninety thousand six hundred eighty-seven

_____

 Explain how to solve the following problem.
1,564 + 4,322 =

Fluency Blast

Practice using mental math.

4	7	10	6	3	9	2	8	5	10	1	3
× 6	× 3	× 8	× 6	× 5	× 7	× 5	× 4	× 5	× 3	× 4	× 2

○○○○

Day 1

1. Rewrite in standard form.

   three hundred fifty-nine thousand six

   _____

2. Write <, >, or = to make the statement true.

   54,686 ◯ 54,989

3. Round each number to the nearest ten. Add.

   212 + 87 is about _____ .

4. $7,676
   + $4,444
   _____

5. Are $\frac{1}{2}$ and $\frac{2}{8}$ equivalent fractions? _____

Day 2

1. Determine the 16th shape in the pattern.

   _____

2. Jack runs 3 miles 4 times a week. How many miles does Jack run in 6 weeks?

   _____

3. List the factors of **19**. _____

   Is **19** prime or composite? _____

4. Blair placed 99 books on a shelf. Of the books, 29 were nonfiction, 12 were poetry, and the rest were fiction. How many books were fiction?

   _____

Day 3

1. 33 m = _____ cm

2. 14 km = _____ m

3. 47 m = _____ mm

4. 900 cm = _____ m

Day 4

1. Draw a right angle.

2. Draw perpendicular lines.

3. What is this an example of?

   ←————————→

   ←————————→

   _____

1. 452,936 + 453,256 = _____

2.   7,495
   − 6,896

3. Rewrite in standard form.

   4 ten thousands, 1 thousand, 9 hundreds, 8 tens, and 4 ones

   _____

4. Round **713,923** to the nearest hundred.

   _____

5. List the factors of **30**. _____

   Is **30** prime or composite? _____

6. Determine the 26th shape in the pattern.

   _____

7. 15 m = _____ cm

8. What kind of angle is shown?

    _____

 Explain how you decide which of two numbers is the greatest.

Fluency Blast

Practice using mental math.

2	9	3	5	7	4	0	6	1	8	10	6
× 2	× 4	× 7	× 9	× 6	× 3	× 5	× 9	× 2	× 3	×10	× 0

Day 1

1. 15,545
    + 26,345

2. 499
    +427

3. Rewrite in standard form.

   400,000 + 8,000 + 500 + 3

   _____

4. Are these equivalent fractions? _____

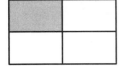 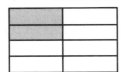

5. Write <, >, or = to make the statement true.

   121,453 ◯ 112,678

Day 2

1. List the factors of **39**. _____

   Is **39** prime or composite? _____

2. Write the missing numbers to complete the pattern.

   615, 605, 595, _____, _____,

   _____, _____, _____

3. A can holds 75 marbles. Every hour, 17 marbles are taken out. After 4 hours, how many marbles are left? _____

4. Eleven spiders are building webs in the barn. Each spider has 8 legs. How many spider legs are there in all?

   _____

Day 3

1. Mia and her family reach the amusement park at 8:15. They wait in line to enter the park for 55 minutes. What time do they go in?

   _____

2. How many inches long is the feather?

 _____

3. 5 km = _____ m

4. 84 cm = _____ mm

Day 4

1. What kind of lines are shown?

   _____

2. Draw an acute angle.

3. Which word describes the triangle?

   A. equilateral   B. isosceles   C. scalene

1. On Monday, 32 pencils are in a basket. If 6 pencils are taken out of the basket each day until Friday, how many pencils will be left in the basket on Friday?

   _____

2. List the factors of **17**. _____

   Is **17** prime or composite? _____

3. Write the fraction.

   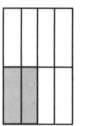 _____

4. Write <, >, or = to make the statement true.

   786,544 $\bigcirc$ 786,454

5. 27,791
   − 23,182

6. How many inches long is the toothbrush?

   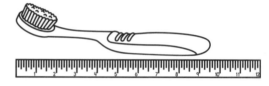

   _____

7. The basketball game began at 7:05. The game took 3 hours and 15 minutes to play. What time did the basketball game end? _____

8. 8 km = _____ m

 Explain how place value helps you understand the different values of the 2 in 20, 200, and 2,000.

Name _____

Fluency Blast

Practice using mental math.

26	68	54	47	83	49	52	86	72	32	58	35
× 2	× 3	× 5	× 8	× 9	× 7	× 9	× 6	× 8	× 3	× 3	× 6

○○○○

Day 1

1. 15 + 39 + 10 = _____

2. Write a related multiplication fact.

   5 + 5 + 5 _____

3. Write <, >, or = to make the statement true.

   649 ◯ 694

4. Rewrite in standard form.

   60,000 + 5,000 + 500 + 7

   _____

5.   77,528
     − 68,431
     ‾‾‾‾‾‾‾

Day 2

1. List the factors of **14**. _____

   Is **14** prime or composite? _____

2. Complete the table.

× 3, − 6	
5	9
6	
7	
8	
9	

Day 3

1. A pool for the elephants needs 79 liters of water. How many milliliters of water are needed? _____

2. Benji is making punch and needs 4,000 milliliters of pineapple juice. How many liters of juice does he need?

   _____

3. 5 cm = _____ mm

Day 4

1. Color the shapes that have 4 vertices.

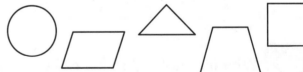

2. Draw an obtuse angle.

3. Which word describes the triangle?

   A. equilateral   B. isosceles   C. scalene

Name _____

1. Complete the table.

× 2, – 1	
4	7
5	
6	
7	
8	

2. List the factors of **24**. _____

   Is **24** prime or composite? _____

3. 353,816
   + 240,210

4. Write the missing numbers to complete the pattern.

   203, 206, 209, _____, _____,

   _____, _____, _____

5. 10 cm = _____ mm

6. 216,965 – 104,426 _____

7. Anna needs liters of ginger ale and cola for a party, but the bottles are only labeled in milliliters. If she buys 40,000 milliliters of ginger ale and 30,000 milliliters of cola, how many liters will she have altogether?

   _____

8. What kind of angle is shown?

   _____

Why is it helpful to be able to convert numbers between standard form, word form, and expanded form?

Fluency Blast

Practice using mental math.

42	35	44	13	7	4	63	24	52	48	91	38
× 9	× 4	× 2	× 3	× 11	× 22	× 4	× 3	× 8	× 5	× 3	× 9

Day 1

1. 543,886
   + 89,909

2. 857
   −648

3. Write <, >, or = to make the statement true.

   87,877 ◯ 877,555

4. Rewrite in standard form.

   ninety-five thousand one hundred seventy-five

   _____

5. Write a related multiplication fact.

   54 ÷ 6 = 9 _____

Day 2

1. List the factors of **36**. _____

   Is **36** prime or composite? _____

2. Determine the 12th shape in the pattern.

   _____

3. Mr. Chu buys 54 flowers. He puts 6 flowers in each vase. If he sells each vase for $3, how much money does he earn? _____

4. Gerardo has 36 golf clubs. He has 3 golf bags. Each bag contains the same number of clubs. How many clubs are in each bag?

   _____

Day 3

1. 90 mm = _____ cm

2. 600 mm = _____ cm

3. 11 cm = _____ mm

4. 7 km = _____ m

5. 400 mm = _____ cm

Day 4

Name each quadrilateral.

1.

   _____

2.

   _____

3.

   _____

4.

   _____

---

1. Allison earned $405 in June and $545 in July. How much money in all did Allison earn in June and July? _____

2. List the factors of **23**. _____

   Is **23** prime or composite? _____

3. Rewrite in expanded form.

   2,124

   _____

4. 14,643
   – 13,299
   _____

5. Quan has 90 golf balls to put into buckets. He puts 5 golf balls into each bucket. How many buckets did Quan use?

   _____

6. Write <, >, or = to make the statement true.

   3,864 ◯ 3,864

7. Determine the 22nd shape in the pattern.

   _____

8. 23 km = _____ m

 Show two different ways to solve the problem. 5 × 5 × 4 = Which way is easiest for you? Why?

Fluency Blast

Practice using mental math.

57	23	3	67	8	3	72	58	42	90	27	52
× 2	× 7	× 71	× 7	× 19	× 51	× 8	× 5	× 9	× 4	× 4	× 2

○○○○

Day 1

1. Write <, >, or = to make the statement true.

$$\frac{1}{8} \bigcirc \frac{5}{8}$$

2.
```
  293,422        576
+ 292,434       +498
```

3. Rewrite in standard form.

80,000 + 7,000 + 400 + 70 + 8

_____

4.
```
  87,223
− 86,224
```

Day 2

1. List the factors of **20**. _____

   Is **20** prime or composite? _____

2. On the day she was born, a baby leopard had 12 spots. Each day, 4 more spots appeared. After 5 days, how many spots did the baby leopard have? (Hint: Draw a T-chart.)

   _____

3. Complete the pattern.

   1, 2, 4, 7, 11, 16, 22, _____, _____,

   _____, _____

Day 3

1. An average-sized dog weighs about

   A. 15 grams.   B. 50 grams.

   C. 500 grams.   D. 15,000 grams.

2. Terrance parks his car at 4:08. He wants to visit the bookstore, so he puts enough money in the parking meter for $1\frac{1}{2}$ hours. What time should he be back at his car? _____

3. 9,000 m = _____ km

4. 10,000 m = _____ km

Day 4

1. Is every square a quadrilateral? _____

   Why or why not? _____

   _____

2. Draw a straight angle.

3. Caleb cut a shape out of a sheet of paper. The shape had 4 sides, with opposite sides parallel. What shape could Caleb have cut out?

   A. hexagon   B. parallelogram

   C. equilateral triangle

1. List the factors of **33**. _____
   Is **33** prime or composite? _____

2. Write the missing numbers to complete the pattern.
   89, 85, 81, _____, _____, _____
   _____, _____

3. Blane has 42 stickers. He shares 5 stickers with his friends every day. After 5 days, how many stickers will Blane have left? (Hint: Draw a T-chart.) _____

4. Rewrite in expanded form.
   259,341
   _____

5.   14,243
    + 41,208
      ‾‾‾‾‾‾‾

6. Round **12,567** to the nearest thousand.
   _____

7. A nail weighs about
   A. 1 gram.　　　B. 10 grams.
   C. 100 grams.　D. 1,000 grams.

8. 13 km = _____ m

 What are some reasons why rounding is helpful? Which reason do you think is the most helpful?

CD-104974 • © Carson-Dellosa

Fluency Blast

Practice using mental math.

63	17	95	36	20	19	64	78	82	76	53	91
× 8	× 8	× 5	× 5	× 9	× 9	× 2	× 2	× 3	× 8	× 5	× 9

○○○○

Day 1

1. Rewrite in standard form.

   thirty-seven thousand five hundred ninety

   _____

2. 48,644
    +43,987

3. 642,199
    – 624,199

4. Write <, >, or = to make the statement true.

   642,199 ◯ 624,199

5. Solve.

   21 ÷ 3 = _____   24 ÷ 6 = _____

   50 ÷ 10 = _____

Day 2

1. Alvin is 3 years old. His sister is 4 times older. How old is Alvin's sister? _____

2. Complete the table.

× 10	
10	100
11	
12	
13	
14	

Day 3

Find the perimeter of each shape.

1.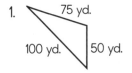
   75 yd.
   100 yd.   50 yd.

   _____

2.
   3 m
   4 m   4 m
   3 m

   _____

3.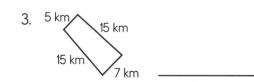
   5 km   15 km
   15 km
   7 km   _____

Day 4

Identify each triangle as **scalene**, **isosceles**, or **equilateral**.

1.

   _____

2.

   _____

3.

   _____

4.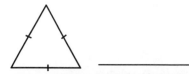

   _____

Name _____

1. Ursula filled all 25 shelves in her room with books. She placed 7 books on each shelf. How many books did she place on all 25 shelves?

   _____

2. Round **634,121** to the nearest ten thousand.

   _____

3. Find the perimeter.

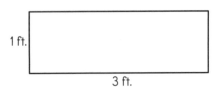

   _____

4. Complete the table.

× 5	
5	25
6	
7	
8	
9	

5. Yolanda has 4 hair bows. Her sister has 6 times as many hair bows as Yolanda. How many hair bows does Yolanda's sister have?

   _____

6. Draw scalene, isosceles, and equilateral triangles. Label them.

7. Find the perimeter.

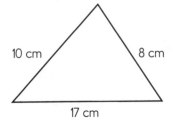

   _____

8. Hunter took 67 photos of landmarks in the city he visited. He took 13 photos of buildings, 18 photos of bridges, and 2 photos of statues. The rest were photos of parks. How many photos of parks did Hunter take?

   _____

 Compare and contrast what makes a triangle scalene, isosceles, or equilateral. Draw examples of each. Label the differences.

 CD-104974 • © Carson-Dellosa

Fluency Blast

Practice using mental math.

12	33	48	75	98	70	43	56	22	55	73	42
× 4	× 2	× 9	× 3	× 6	× 7	× 2	× 5	× 3	× 8	× 2	× 8

○○○○

Day 1

1. Rewrite in standard form.

   800,000 + 20,000 + 7,000 + 600 + 70 + 2

   _____

2. 39
   × 7

3. 87
   × 5

4. 73,886
   + 51,313

5. 74,462
   − 73,861

Day 2

1. Victor mows 1 lawn every day Monday through Saturday. He is paid $25 for each lawn. How much money does Victor earn in 2 weeks of mowing lawns? _____

2. Sixty-five students voted for Jessica. Two times as many students voted for Sierra. How many students voted in all? _____

3. Write the missing numbers to complete the pattern.

   100, 99, 97, 94, 90, 85, _____, _____,

   _____, _____, _____

Day 3

1. A swimming pool has a perimeter of 80 feet. The short sides measure 16 feet each. What is the length of the longer sides of the pool?

   _____

2. The area of a window measures 352 square inches. If the window is 16 inches wide, how tall is the window? _____

3. Find the area.

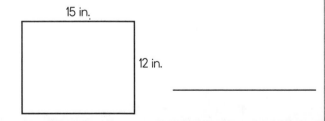

15 in.

12 in.

_____

Day 4

Name each angle. Then, identify it as **right**, **acute**, or **obtuse**.

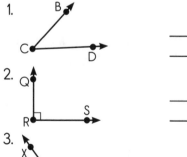

1.   B
   C   D

   _____

   _____

2. Q
   R   S

   _____

   _____

3. X
   Y   Z

   _____

   _____

4.

   P
   R   Q

   _____

   _____

1. Twenty-six people voted for fish as their favorite pet. Three times as many people voted for dogs. How many people voted in all?

   _____

2. 69
   × 9
   ___

3. 94
   × 4
   ___

4. Spencer eats 39 animal crackers as a snack every day after school. How many animal crackers does he eat during a 5-day school week? _____

5. A rectangular blanket's perimeter is 250 inches. If two sides of the blanket measures 60 inches, what is the length of the other sides of the blanket?

   _____

6. The door to the clubhouse has an area of 2,016 square centimeters. If the length of the door is 56 centimeters, what is the width of the door?

   _____

7. The town hall's bell rings 12 times every hour. How many times does the bell ring in a 24-hour period? _____

8. Find the area.

   12 mm

   12 mm

   _____

 Explain the difference between finding perimeter and area. What is a real-world situation where you might need to find perimeter?

Fluency Blast

Practice using mental math.

32	90	22	12	11	20	75	11	30	15	13	12
× 2	× 1	× 4	× 3	× 9	× 5	× 1	× 6	× 3	× 2	× 3	× 4

○○○○

Day 1

1. 153 ÷ 3 = _____

2. Rewrite in standard form.

   seventeen thousand nine hundred thirty-four

   _____

3.   183,982
   + 281,294
   _____

4. 7,489 − 6,726 = _____

5.   232
   ×   4
   _____

Day 2

1. List the factors of **59**. _____

   Is **59** prime or composite? _____

2. Taron unpacked 47 boxes of light bulbs for the discount warehouse. Each box contained 6 bulbs. How many bulbs were in the 47 boxes?

   _____

3. Zoe's hair is 5 inches long. If her hair grows 2 inches each month, how long will her hair be after 6 months? _____

Day 3

1. The perimeter of a rectangular yard is 214 feet. If the width of the yard is 45 feet, what is the length of the yard? _____

2. The area of the rectangular roof on a dollhouse is 954 square inches. The length of the roof is 106 inches. What is the width of the roof?

   _____

3. Find the area.

   7 in.

   4 in.

   _____

Day 4

Draw a check mark on each polygon. Cross out the shapes that are not polygons.

---

1. 335
   ×   7

2. Erin is 32 inches tall. If she grows 5 inches every year, how tall will she be in three years?

   _____

3. The perimeter of the picture frame is 102 centimeters. The length of the frame is 18 centimeters. What is the width?

   _____

4. 184 ÷ 2 = _____

5. Delinda practiced her flute for half an hour each day for 7 days. How many total minutes did she practice? _____

6. The area of a room in the dollhouse is 1,248 square inches. The width of the room is 32 inches. How long is the room?

   _____

7. Evelyn played her new music for 3 hours every day for the first 5 days she had it. She played it for 1 hour for the next 4 days. How many total minutes did she play her new music?

   _____

8. Jeff walked 4 miles a day for 24 days. How many miles did he walk? _____

 Explain how to convert yards to inches and hours to minutes.

Fluency Blast

Practice using mental math.

3⟌15   4⟌12   5⟌30   4⟌32   3⟌24   2⟌16   7⟌28   9⟌18   9⟌45   7⟌63

○○○○

Day 1

1.   774
   × 3

2.   141
   × 2

3. 288 ÷ 8 = _____

4.   67,987
   − 38,998

5. 868 ÷ 4 = _____

Day 2

1. Complete the table.

+ 4, × 2	
4	16
6	
8	
10	
12	

2. Grantsville's mayor received 5 times as many votes as Cary's mayor. Cary's mayor received 738 votes. How many people voted altogether?

   _____

Day 3

1. Jarvis planted grass in a rectangular space behind the clubhouse. The area of the space is 78 square feet. If the length of the space is 13 feet, what is the width of the space?

   _____

2. A rectangular closet has a perimeter of 20 feet. If the width of the closet is 6 feet, what is the length of the closet?

   _____

3. The area of a rectangle is 124 square meters. If the length of the rectangle is 4 meters, what is the width of the rectangle?

   _____

Day 4

Circle the closed shapes. Cross out the open shapes.

1. Nellie made 24 blueberry muffins. If each muffin contained 6 blueberries, how many total blueberries did Nellie use?

   _____

2. 639 × 11 = _____

3. Six times as many people voted in the 2012 local election as in the 2008 local election. If 192 people voted in 2008, how many people voted in 2012?

   _____

4. A rectangular bedroom has a perimeter of 42 feet. The length is 13 feet. What is the width?

   _____

5. Complete the table.

× 5, + 2	
2	12
4	
6	
8	
10	

6. Lamar made 5 batches of biscuits. He made 24 biscuits in each batch. How many biscuits did he make in all?

   _____

7. The area of a bathroom floor is 24 square feet. If the width of the bathroom is 3 feet, what is the length of the bathroom?

   _____

8. Draw and label one open shape and one closed shape.

You have to find the area of your classroom. You do not have a ruler or a yardstick. How could you measure the room? How would you determine if you had chosen a good measuring device?

Fluency Blast

Practice using mental math.

$7\overline{)49}$ $5\overline{)45}$ $6\overline{)36}$ $3\overline{)24}$ $3\overline{)27}$ $2\overline{)12}$ $6\overline{)60}$ $7\overline{)56}$ $7\overline{)42}$ $6\overline{)24}$

○○○○

Day 1

1.   413,206
    − 178,598

2.   325,211
    + 188,456

3. 774 ÷ 6 = _____

4. Rewrite in standard form.
    nine thousand eight hundred ninety-two
    _____

5. Round **268,735** to the nearest hundred.
    _____

Day 2

1. Mischa has saved $61. Ty has saved 3 times as much money as Mischa. How much money has Ty saved? _____

2. Complete the table.

− 8	
1,000	992
1,001	
1,002	
1,003	
1,004	

3. List the factors of **68**. _____
    Is **68** prime or composite? _____

Day 3

Find the perimeter of each shape.

1.
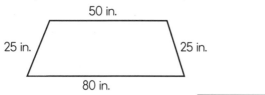
50 in.
25 in.   25 in.
80 in.
_____

2.
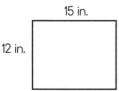
15 in.
12 in.
_____

3.
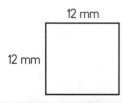
12 mm
12 mm
_____

Day 4

Color the shapes that have parallel lines.
Circle the shapes that have perpendicular lines.

1. 4,214
    ×   8
    _____

2. Rewrite in standard form.

    three hundred forty-two thousand six hundred eight

    _____

3. 68,242
    +38,254
    _____

4. List the factors of **67**. _____

    Is **67** prime or composite? _____

5. Katherine spends 7 hours at the gym each week. How much time does she spend at the gym in an 8-week period? _____

6. A sold-out concert is playing at Twilight Pavilion on Friday, Saturday, and Sunday nights. A total of 729 tickets were sold for each night of the performances. How many tickets were sold for the 3 nights? _____

7. Find the perimeter.

    10 yd.

    25 yd.

    _____

8. How many sets of sides are parallel in an octagon? _____

 Compare and contrast the attributes of a square and a rhombus.

Fluency Blast

Practice using mental math.

$8\overline{)56}$ $6\overline{)48}$ $6\overline{)30}$ $4\overline{)32}$ $7\overline{)35}$ $9\overline{)63}$ $5\overline{)25}$ $7\overline{)21}$ $8\overline{)40}$ $9\overline{)90}$

○○○○

Day 1

1. 173,326
    + 161,288
    _____

2. 754,326
    − 656,245
    _____

3. $92 \times 17 =$ _____ $140 \div 4 =$ _____

4. Rewrite in word form.

    50,328

    _____

    _____

5. Round **462,145** to the nearest ten.

    _____

Day 2

1. A total of 405 students will attend Field Day. Mr. Wolf needs 4 ribbons for each student and 36 ribbons for the parents who will be helping. How many ribbons does Mr. Wolf need in all?

    _____

2. Complete the table.

+13	
92	105
95	
98	
101	
104	

Day 3

1. The area of a rectangular ice-skating rink is 900 square yards. If the length of the rink is 90 yards, what is the width of the rink?

    _____

2. The perimeter of a sheet of paper is 28 centimeters. If the width of the paper is 8 centimeters, what is the length of the paper?

    _____

3. Draw square units to show the area of the rectangle.

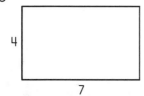

Day 4

Circle the triangles. Color the quadrilaterals.

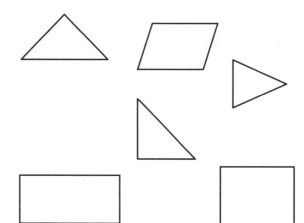

1. 324,159
   − 228,634

2. 105 ÷ 8 = _____

3. Rewrite in word form.

   505,205

   _____

   _____

4. Kennedy earns $9 each time she babysits her little sister. If Kennedy babysits her sister 7 times, how much money will she earn? _____

5. Nadia, Jimmy, and Terry collected 769 stickers during the school year. They want to divide the stickers equally. They plan to give any leftover stickers to Vanessa. How many stickers will Nadia, Jimmy, and Terry get?

   _____

6. Round **10,990** to the nearest hundred.

   _____

7. The area of Brooke's vegetable garden is 40 square feet. If the width of the garden is 8 feet, what is the length of the garden?

   _____

8. Draw one triangle and one quadrilateral. Label the parts.

 Is a trapezoid a parallelogram? Explain your reasoning.

Fluency Blast

Practice using mental math.

$5\overline{)35}$ $4\overline{)16}$ $4\overline{)36}$ $3\overline{)18}$ $5\overline{)25}$ $2\overline{)14}$ $5\overline{)45}$ $4\overline{)24}$ $2\overline{)12}$ $5\overline{)50}$

○○○○

Day 1

1. Rewrite in standard form.

   eight hundred twenty-one thousand nine hundred four

   _____

2. Round **263,548** to the nearest hundred thousand. _____

3.   543,296
   $-$ 211,790

4. Write <, >, or = to make the statement true.

   94,305 ◯ 94,360

5. 2,002 × 4 = _____   1,002 ÷ 2 = _____

Day 2

1. The movie theater had 416 people in it. If the people split into 8 even groups to watch different movies, how many people will watch each movie? _____

2. Determine the 30th shape in the pattern.

   _____

3. List the factors of **75**. _____

   Is **75** prime or composite? _____

Day 3

Find the area of each shape.

1.

   7 in.

   4 in.

   _____

2.
   15 in.

   12 in.

   _____

3.
   20 km

   4 km

   _____

Day 4

Place a check mark on each shape that is regular. Cross out the shapes that are irregular.

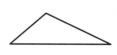

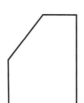

1. $4{,}912 \div 2 =$ _____

2. Round **743,314** to the nearest ten thousand.

    _____

3. $\begin{array}{r} 49{,}320 \\ + 56{,}243 \\ \hline \end{array}$

4. The movie theater donated 675 tickets to 9 schools. If the movie theater donated the same number of tickets to each school, how many tickets did each school receive?

    _____

5. A blue whale traveled 498 feet the first time he was sighted. The second time he was sighted, the blue whale had traveled 8 times as far as the first time. How far did the blue whale travel altogether? _____

6. The perimeter of a rectangle is 164 feet. The length of the rectangle is 55 feet. What is the width of the rectangle? _____

7. Find the area.

    15 mm

    15 mm

    _____

8. Draw a regular shape that has 4 sides. Draw an irregular shape that has 4 sides.

 Explain the difference between a prime number and a composite number.

Fluency Blast

Practice using mental math.

8)‾4‾0‾   8)‾4‾8‾   6)‾4‾2‾   3)‾2‾7‾   7)‾5‾6‾   9)‾1‾8‾   7)‾4‾2‾   9)‾8‾1‾   9)‾7‾2‾   7)‾3‾5‾

○○○○

Day 1

1. Rewrite in standard form.

   eight hundred sixty thousand nine hundred fifteen

   _____

2. 624,193
   + 252,126
   _____

3. Round **267,596** to the nearest thousand.

   _____

4. Write <, >, or = to make the statement true.

   62,381 ◯ 62,831

5. 92 × 22 = _____   224 ÷ 5 = _____

Day 2

1. Macon saw 4 times as many footballs as soccer balls in the store. Macon saw 234 soccer balls. How many footballs did he see?

   _____

2. Complete the table.

× 4	
12	48
13	
14	
15	
16	

Day 3

1. The perimeter of the top of a desk is 58 inches. If the length of the desk is 15 inches, what is the width of the desk? _____

2. The area of a rectangle is 336 square inches. The width of the rectangle is 14 inches. What is the length of the rectangle?

   _____

3. The perimeter of the cover of a math textbook is 34 inches. If the width of the cover is 9 inches, what is the length of the cover?

   _____

Day 4

Color the convex polygons. Circle the concave polygons.

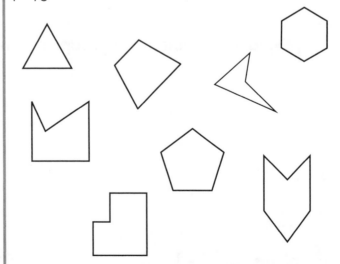

1. 743,245
   − 668,195

2. Round **329,167** to the nearest hundred.

   _____

3. Rewrite in standard form.

   forty-three thousand sixteen

   _____

4. In winter, a sporting goods store sells 12 times as many snowboards as it sells during summer. The store sells 132 snowboards in summer. How many snowboards does the store sell in winter?

   _____

5. Noah rides bikes 13 miles a day, 5 days a week. How many miles does Noah bike in 8 weeks?

   _____

6. 768 ÷ 4 = _____

7. The perimeter of a deck is 38 feet. If the length of the deck is 10 feet, what is the width of the deck? _____

8. Draw one convex shape and one concave shape. Label each.

 Explain how you use regrouping to help you add or subtract.

Fluency Blast

Practice using mental math.

8 × 49	52 × 3	34 × 3	17 × 5	35 × 5
54 ÷ 9	21 ÷ 3	28 ÷ 7	18 ÷ 3	45 ÷ 5

○○○○

Day 1

1. 6,312 ÷ 8 = _____

2. Round **241,558** to the nearest ten.

   _____

3. Rewrite in word form.

   841,504

   _____

   _____

4. 75   38
   × 49   × 25

5. 753,091
   + 773,256

Day 2

1. The area of the top of a rectangular table is 342 square feet. If the length of the table is 19 feet, what is the width of the table?

   _____

2. Complete the table.

× 7	
7	49
8	
9	
10	
11	

Day 3

Find the perimeter.

1.
   6 ft.
   6 ft.   6 ft.
   6 ft.

   _____

2. 13 cm   13 cm
   2 cm

   _____

3.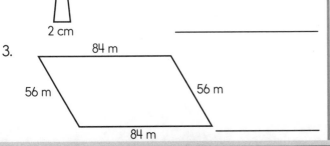
   84 m
   56 m   56 m
   84 m

   _____

Day 4

Circle the polygons that have perpendicular lines.

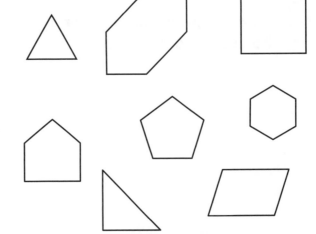

1. Lynn earned $37 each week for delivering newspapers. She delivered newspapers for 2 weeks. How much money did Lynn earn?

   _____

2. 23   31
   $\times\,40$ $\times\,30$

3.   880,372
    $-\,851,684$

4. The area of a dog kennel is 28 square feet. If the length of the kennel is 4 feet, what is the width of the kennel? _____

5. Round **463,462** to the nearest ten thousand.

   _____

6. Rewrite in standard form.

   900,000 + 20,000 + 2,000 + 100 + 7

   _____

7. Find the perimeter.

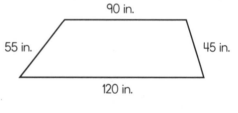

8. Draw an octagon that has perpendicular lines.

 If the length of the dog kennel in problem 4 were doubled, how would that change the area? Why?

Fluency Blast

Practice using mental math.

36 ÷ 9	42 ÷ 6	64 ÷ 8	84 ÷ 3	64 ÷ 4
7 × 90	8 × 21	9 × 15	5 × 33	7 × 19

○○○○

Day 1

1.
$$\begin{array}{r} 58 \\ \times\ 15 \\ \hline \end{array}$$
$$\begin{array}{r} 72 \\ \times\ 30 \\ \hline \end{array}$$

2. Round **2,517** to the nearest hundred.

   _____

3.
$$\begin{array}{r} 482,122 \\ +\ 512,137 \\ \hline \end{array}$$

4. Write <, >, or = to make the statement true.

   603,897 ◯ 630.897

5. What is $\frac{1}{2}$ of 46? _____

Day 2

1. Travis had a party and invited 12 friends. He had 360 baseball cards to give away as party favors. How many baseball cards did each friend receive if Travis gave away all of his cards?

   _____

2. Complete the table.

+ 8	
158	166
159	
160	
161	
162	

Day 3

1. Find the perimeter.

   _____

2. Find the area.

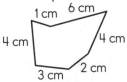

   _____

3. Find the area.

   1 m ▭
   20 m

   _____

Day 4

Write **A**, **R**, or **O** in each angle to identify it as **acute**, **right**, or **obtuse**.

---

1. Nadia buys 15 picture frames for $12 each, including tax. If Nadia has $190, how much change will she get back after she buys the picture frames? _____

2. 42 × 33   90 ÷ 9

3. Round **608,897** to the nearest ten.

   _____

4. The perimeter of a picture frame is 28 inches. If the width of the picture frame is 6 inches, what is the length of the picture frame?

   _____

5. On each table, Lola displayed 14 crafts. If she had 8 tables, how many crafts did she display?

   _____

6. Write <, >, or = to make the statement true.

   136,284 ◯ 134,284

7. Find the perimeter.

   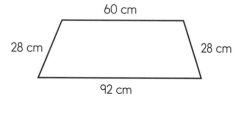

   60 cm

   28 cm   28 cm

   92 cm

   _____

8. Draw a hexagon that has two right angles. Draw a hexagon that has two acute angles.

 In problem 4, the picture frame's perimeter is 28 inches. What happens to the length if the width is decreased to 3 inches? Show your thinking.

CD-104974 • © Carson-Dellosa

Fluency Blast

Practice using mental math.

800 × 10	30 × 10	9,000 × 10	4,000 × 10	50,000 × 10
70 × 10	100 × 10	4 × 10	500 × 10	8,000 × 10

○ ○ ○ ○

Day 1

1. $\frac{3}{5}$
   $+ \frac{1}{5}$

2. If $\frac{3}{10} = \frac{30}{100}$, then $\frac{4}{10} = \frac{}{100}$.

3. $3\frac{1}{3}$
   $+ 2\frac{1}{3}$

4. If $\frac{6}{10} = 0.6$, then $\frac{5}{10} =$ _____.

Day 2

1. Complete the table.

× 5	
4	20
5	
6	
7	
8	

2. If it takes Monique $\frac{1}{4}$ of an hour to do her homework, and it takes Miguel $\frac{3}{4}$ of an hour to do his homework, how much time does it take Monique and Miguel to do their homework altogether? _____

   How much longer does it take Miguel to do his homework than Monique? _____

Day 3

Use the line plot to answer the questions.

Lengths of Books on a Shelf (in.)

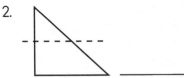

1. How many books are on the shelf altogether?
   _____

2. What is the difference between the longest and shortest books? _____

3. How many books on the shelf are at least 6 inches long? _____

Day 4

Determine if the line drawn on each shape is a line of symmetry and write **yes** or **no**.

1. 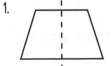 _____

2. 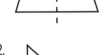 _____

3. 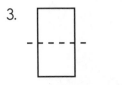 _____

Name _____

1. $\dfrac{1}{3}$

    $+\ \dfrac{1}{3}$

2. If $\dfrac{2}{10} = \dfrac{20}{100}$, then $\dfrac{5}{10} = \dfrac{}{100}$.

3. If it takes Nora $\dfrac{3}{4}$ of an hour to clean a bathroom, and it takes Owen $\dfrac{1}{4}$ of an hour to clean a bathroom, how much total time does it take Nora and Owen to clean the bathrooms?

    _____

4. If $\dfrac{4}{10} = 0.4$, then $\dfrac{8}{10} = $ _____.

5. $4\dfrac{2}{5}$

    $+\ \dfrac{1}{5}$

6. Krystal won 8 tickets. Rashad won 8 times as many tickets as Krystal. How many tickets did Rashad win? _____

7. Determine if the line drawn on the shape is a line of symmetry and write **yes** or **no**.

    _____   _____

8. Draw a line of symmetry.

 Explain why the fractions are equivalent.

$\dfrac{6}{8} = \dfrac{9}{12}$

Fluency Blast

Practice using mental math.

$4,000 \div 10$	$70 \div 10$	$20,000 \div 10$	$90,000 \div 10$	$100,000 \div 10$
$200 \div 10$	$70,000 \div 10$	$9,000 \div 10$	$40,000 \div 10$	$600,000 \div 10$

Day 1

1. Write <, >, or = to make the statement true.

2.
$$\frac{1}{6}$$
$$+\ \frac{2}{6}$$

3. Round **543,878** to the nearest ten thousand.

_____

4. If $\frac{3}{10} = \frac{30}{100}$, then $\frac{8}{10} = \frac{}{100}$.

5. If $\frac{4}{10} + \frac{5}{100} = \frac{45}{100}$, then $\frac{7}{10} + \frac{7}{100} = \frac{}{100}$.

Day 2

1. The area of a rectangle is 1,176 square meters. The width of the rectangle is 21 meters. What is the length of the rectangle?

_____

2. The brown horse runs $\frac{3}{12}$ of a mile. The black horse runs $\frac{4}{12}$ of a mile. How many miles total do the black and brown horses run?

_____

3. The perimeter of a rectangle is 60 meters. If the length of the rectangle is 14 meters, what is the width of the rectangle? _____

Day 3

Complete the line plot. Answer the questions.

Flour Used in Cookie Recipes				
$4\frac{1}{2}$	||	6		
5	|||	$6\frac{1}{2}$		||
$5\frac{1}{2}$	|	7		

Flour Used (c.)

1. What is the total number of cookie recipes?

_____

2. How many recipes call for $4\frac{1}{2}$ cups of flour?

_____

Day 4

Label each shape as **symmetrical** or **nonsymmetrical**. If the shape is symmetrical, draw one line of symmetry.

1.

_____

2.

_____

3.

_____

1. Write <, >, or = to make the statement true.

2. If $\frac{16}{100}$ = 0.16, then $\frac{87}{100}$ = _____.

3. Round **687,155** to the nearest ten.

    _____

4. Nell runs $\frac{5}{10}$ of a mile, and Vincent runs $\frac{4}{10}$ of a mile. How many total miles do they run?

    _____

5. $2\frac{4}{5}$

    $+\ \ 3\frac{2}{5}$

6. If $\frac{5}{10} = \frac{50}{100}$, then $\frac{9}{10} = \frac{}{100}$.

7. If $\frac{1}{10} + \frac{1}{100} = \frac{11}{100}$, then $\frac{4}{10} + \frac{8}{100} = \frac{}{100}$.

8. Label the shape as **symmetrical** or **nonsymmetrical**.

    _____

 Compare a pictograph to a line plot. How are they alike? How are they different? When would it be better to use a pictograph? When would it be better to use a line plot?

Fluency Blast

Practice using mental math.

6,000 × 100	70,000 × 100	800 × 100	2,000 × 100	340 × 100
450 × 100	52 × 100	4 × 100	100,000 × 100	280,000 × 100

○○○○

Day 1

1. Decompose in two ways.

$$\frac{3}{8} + \frac{}{8} = \frac{7}{8}$$

$$\frac{2}{8} + \frac{}{8} = \frac{7}{8}$$

2. $\frac{1}{12}$

    $+ \frac{4}{12}$
    _____

3. If $\frac{71}{100} = 0.71$, then $\frac{49}{100} =$ _____.

4. If $\frac{5}{10} = \frac{50}{100}$, then $\frac{6}{10} = \frac{}{100}$.

5. If $\frac{3}{10} + \frac{6}{100} = \frac{36}{100}$, then $\frac{8}{10} + \frac{3}{100} = \frac{}{100}$.

Day 2

1. Pedro orders 595 candy bars. They come in 7 boxes. How many candy bars are in each box? _____

2. List the factors of **16**. _____

   Is **16** prime or composite? _____

3. Cameron adds $\frac{5}{8}$ of a cup of applesauce to his cake recipe. He then measures and adds $\frac{1}{8}$ of a cup more of applesauce. How much applesauce has Cameron added to his cake altogether? _____

Day 3

Use the line plot to answer the questions.

Lengths of Ribbons in a Bag (in.)

```
                        X
 X                   X  X
 X                   X  X
 X     X     X    X  X  X
 X     X     X    X  X  X
 X     X     X    X  X  X
 +-----+-----+----+-----+---->
 6    6½     7   7½     8
```

1. How many ribbons are in the bag? _____

2. What is the difference between the longest and shortest ribbons? _____

3. How many ribbons are $6\frac{1}{2}$ inches long?
   _____

Day 4

1. Circle the triangle that shows a line of symmetry.

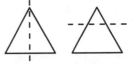

2. Draw a line of symmetry for each shape.

Name _____

1. List the factors of **34**. _____

   Is **34** prime or composite? _____

2. If $\dfrac{4}{10} = \dfrac{40}{100}$, then $\dfrac{7}{10} = \dfrac{}{100}$.

3. If $\dfrac{55}{100} = 0.55$, then $\dfrac{64}{100} =$ _____.

4. A cake recipe calls for $\dfrac{3}{4}$ of a cup of sugar and $\dfrac{2}{4}$ of a cup of flour. How many total cups of sugar and flour are needed?

   _____

5. $\begin{array}{r} \dfrac{1}{4} \\ + \ \dfrac{1}{4} \\ \hline \end{array}$

6. Mario is 2 years old. His aunt is 12 times his age. How old is Mario's aunt? _____

7. Draw a line of symmetry.

8. Use the line plot to answer the question.

   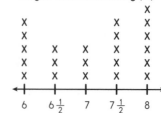

   How many ribbons are 7 or $7\dfrac{1}{2}$ inches long?

   _____

 Use a visual to prove that the math statement is incorrect.

$\dfrac{1}{4} = \dfrac{3}{8}$

 CD-104974 • © Carson-Dellosa

Fluency Blast

Practice using mental math.

60,000 ÷ 10	4,000 ÷ 10	700,000 ÷ 10	500 ÷ 10	28,000 ÷ 10
79,000 ÷ 10	5,240 ÷ 10	582,000 ÷ 10	36,000 ÷ 10	900,000 ÷ 10

Day 1

1. Write the decimal. $\frac{14}{100}$ = _____

2. $\frac{1}{10} + \frac{6}{100} = \frac{}{100}$.

3. Write <, >, or = to make the statement true.

$$\frac{3}{6} \bigcirc \frac{4}{8}$$

4. $2\frac{7}{10}$
   $+ \ 1\frac{1}{10}$
   _____

5. 1,505 ÷ 5 = _____   21 × 31 = _____

Day 2

1. The Lindberg family ate $\frac{2}{6}$ of a pineapple pizza and $\frac{3}{6}$ of a cheese pizza. How much total pizza did the Lindberg family eat? _____

2. The perimeter of a rectangular sandbox is 34 feet. If the length of the sandbox is 8 feet, what is the width of the sandbox?

_____

3. Maggie has 150 key chains. She wants to store an equal number of key chains in 2 containers. How many key chains should she store in each container? _____

Day 3

Judd was watching the weather forecast for a science experiment. Use the graph to answer the questions.

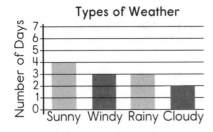

Types of Weather

1. What weather was most likely? _____
2. For how many days did Judd plot the weather?

_____

3. What weather was least likely? _____

Day 4

1. Circle the shape that shows a line of symmetry.

2. Draw a line of symmetry for each shape.

---

1. The Novak family ate $\frac{3}{4}$ of a cheese pizza and $\frac{2}{3}$ of a vegetarian pizza. How much total pizza did the Novak family eat?

_____

2. Write the decimal.

$\frac{32}{100}$ = _____

3. Write <, >, or = to make the statement true.

$\frac{5}{10}$ ◯ $\frac{3}{6}$

4. $\frac{3}{10} + \frac{6}{100} = \frac{}{100}$.

5. 34 × 12 = _____

   876 × 6 = _____

6.
$$3\frac{5}{6}$$
$$+ \; 2\frac{3}{6}$$

7. Draw a line of symmetry.

8. How many more days was the weather sunny than cloudy?

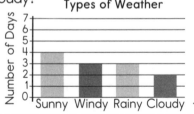

Types of Weather

_____

Why was a bar graph a good choice to collect data for the weather experiment on day 3?

Fluency Blast

Practice using mental math.

5 × 70	4 × 9,000	200,000 × 3	50 × 400	30,000 × 3
3 × 800	9 × 50,000	600 × 900	90 × 2,000	500 × 5

○○○○

Day 1

1. Write the decimal.

   $\frac{54}{100}$ = _____

2. $\frac{9}{10} + \frac{9}{100}$ = _____

3. $5\frac{4}{8}$

   $+ \quad \frac{2}{8}$

   _____

4. Round **320,152** to the nearest ten.

   _____

5. $\frac{3}{12} + \frac{5}{12}$ = _____

Day 2

1. The mayor of Hoffman Hollow gave 3 flags to every person in his community. Hoffman Hollow has 1,294 people. How many flags did the mayor give out? _____

2. Dion ate $\frac{3}{10}$ of a pumpkin pie. Parker ate $\frac{6}{10}$ of the same pie. How much of the pie did Dion and Parker eat altogether?

   _____

3. Zaina's dog weighs 24 pounds. Trey's dog weighs 42 pounds. Chase's dog weighs 2 times as much as Zaina's and Trey's dogs combined. How much does Chase's dog weigh? _____

Day 3

Iesha's class project was to plant trees. Use the graph to answer the questions.

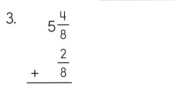

Trees Planted	
Aug.	🌱🌱
Sept.	🌱🌱🌱🌱
Oct.	🌱🌱🌱🌱🌱🌱🌱🌱
Nov.	🌱🌱🌱

🌱 = 4 trees

1. How many more trees were planted in September than November? _____

2. In which month did the class plant the greatest number of trees? _____

3. How many trees did the class plant in all?

   _____

Day 4

1. Circle the shape that shows a line of symmetry.

2. Draw a line of symmetry on each shape.

 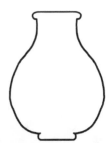

1. Laura ate $\frac{3}{12}$ of a bag of popcorn. Olivia ate $\frac{4}{12}$ of the same bag of popcorn. What fraction of the bag did the girls eat altogether?

_____

2. $\frac{}{10} = \frac{80}{100}$

3.
$$3\frac{7}{12}$$
$$+ \ 4\frac{9}{12}$$

4. Write the decimal.

$\frac{26}{100} =$ _____

5.
$$\frac{6}{8}$$
$$+ \ \frac{1}{8}$$

6. Perry has 135 books. If he places them equally in 3 boxes, how many books are in each box?

_____

How many books will Perry have left if he donates 1 box of books to the library?

_____

7. Draw the line of symmetry.

8.

Trees Planted	
Aug.	🌱🌱
Sept.	🌱🌱🌱🌱
Oct.	🌱🌱🌱🌱🌱🌱🌱
Nov.	🌱🌱🌱

🌱 = 4 trees

How many more trees were planted in November than in August?

_____

 You have an assignment to collect the daily rainfall for two weeks. What would be the best way to collect the data? What would be the best way to display the data? Why did you choose that display?

Fluency Blast

Practice using mental math.

450 ÷ 9	600 ÷ 30	21,000 ÷ 7	900 ÷ 90	30,000 ÷ 300
90 ÷ 9	1,000 ÷ 20	7,000 ÷ 7	900 ÷ 20	22,000 ÷ 11

○○○○

Day 1

1. $\frac{3}{8}$
    $-\frac{1}{8}$

2. $5\frac{1}{3}$
    $-2\frac{2}{3}$

3. Write the decimal.
    $\frac{6}{100} =$ _____

4. $\frac{2}{10} + \frac{5}{100} = \frac{}{100}$.

5. If $\frac{7}{8} = 7 \times \left(\frac{1}{8}\right)$, then $\frac{5}{6} = \boxed{} \times \left(\frac{}{}\right)$.

Day 2

1. List the factors of **90**. _____

    Is **90** prime or composite? _____

2. Roberto's bedroom has a perimeter of 46 feet. If the length of the bedroom is 11 feet, what is the width of the bedroom?

    _____

3. Each person will eat $\frac{2}{3}$ of a pound of turkey, and 8 people will be at dinner. How many pounds of turkey will be needed?

    _____

Day 3

Use the line plot to answer the questions.

Lengths of String (in.)

		X			X	
X	X	X		X	X	
X	X	X	X	X	X	

3    $3\frac{1}{4}$ $3\frac{2}{4}$ $3\frac{3}{4}$ 4 $4\frac{1}{4}$ $4\frac{2}{4}$ $4\frac{3}{4}$ 5

1. What is the total number of string pieces?

    _____

2. How many pieces are $4\frac{2}{4}$ inches long?

    _____

3. What is the difference in length between the longest and the shortest pieces of string?

    _____

Day 4

Draw all of the lines of symmetry.

1.

2.

3.

1. Each student needs $\frac{2}{5}$ of a cup of play dough to build a house. How many cups of play dough are needed for 9 students?

_____

2. $\frac{}{10} = \frac{90}{100}$

3. If $\frac{4}{5} = 4 \times \left(\frac{1}{5}\right)$, then $\frac{6}{10} = \boxed{} \times \left(\frac{}{}\right)$.

4. $2 \times \frac{4}{5} = $ _____

5. $\begin{array}{r} 4\frac{1}{6} \\ -\ 3\frac{5}{6} \\ \hline \end{array}$

6. Samantha took $\frac{2}{8}$ of a pan of brownies. Warren took $\frac{5}{8}$ of a pan of brownies. How much more of the pan of brownies did Warren take than Samantha? _____

7. How many pieces of string were measured?

_____

8. What is the difference between the longest and the shortest pieces of string? _____

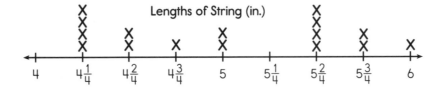

Lengths of String (in.)

 Explain the process you used to list the factors of 90 on day 2. How would the process change if you listed the factors of 91 instead?

CD-104974 • © Carson-Dellosa

Fluency Blast

Practice using mental math. Multiply each number by 2.

20   18   15   12   19   35   30   25   16   11   24   17

○○○○

Day 1

1. Write the decimal.

$\frac{68}{100}$ = _____

2.
$$6\frac{3}{5}$$
$$- 3\frac{1}{5}$$

3.
$$\frac{2}{6}$$
$$- \frac{1}{6}$$

4. If $\frac{9}{10} = 9 \times \left(\frac{1}{10}\right)$, then $\frac{2}{8} = \boxed{} \times \left(\frac{}{}\right)$.

5. $6 \times \frac{1}{5}$ = _____

Day 2

1. Tyler ate $\frac{1}{4}$ of an apple. Brandon ate $\frac{1}{4}$ of the same apple. How much of the apple did the boys eat in all? _____

2. Sandra has 394 paper clips that she has to divide equally between 9 of her coworkers. How many paper clips will each coworker get?

_____

How many paper clips will be left over?

_____

3. Mrs. Xun must give each child $\frac{2}{12}$ of a pizza. She is feeding 4 children. How much pizza does Mrs. Xun need to buy? _____

Day 3

Use the line plot to answer the questions.

Lengths of Sticks (in.)

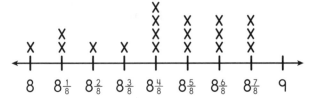

1. How many sticks are there altogether?

_____

2. How many sticks are $8\frac{6}{8}$ inches long? _____

3. What is the difference between the longest stick and the shortest stick? _____

Day 4

Draw all of the lines of symmetry.

1.

2.

3.

1. $\dfrac{3}{10} = \dfrac{}{100}$

2. $\begin{array}{r} 4\frac{7}{10} \\ -\ 3\frac{3}{10} \\ \hline \end{array}$

3. Mr. Lopez must give each child $\dfrac{4}{6}$ of a cup of juice. How much juice in all does Mr. Lopez have to buy for 4 children?

_____

4. $3 \times \dfrac{3}{10} = $ _____

5. Write the decimal.

$\dfrac{29}{100} = $ _____

6. If $\dfrac{4}{5} = 4 \times \left(\dfrac{1}{5}\right)$, then $\dfrac{2}{4} = \boxed{} \times \left(\dfrac{}{}\right).$

7. How long is the longest stick? _____

8. How many sticks were measured?

_____

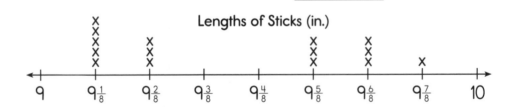

Lengths of Sticks (in.)

 Explain how to change an improper fraction into a mixed number.

Name _____

 Fluency Blast

Practice using mental math. Multiply each number by 3.

20   8   15   12   9   5   30   25   6   11   4   7

○○○○

Day 1

1. Decompose in two ways.

$$\frac{}{10} + \frac{}{10} = \frac{9}{10}$$

$$\frac{}{10} + \frac{}{10} = \frac{9}{10}$$

2. 0.89 ◯ 0.98

3.
$$8\frac{4}{5}$$
$$-\ 5\frac{2}{5}$$
_____

4.
$$\frac{7}{12}$$
$$-\ \frac{5}{12}$$
_____

Day 2

1. Complete the table.

× 4	
4	16
5	
6	
7	
8	

2. Evan shared $\frac{5}{8}$ of his orange with his friend and ate the rest. How much of the orange did Evan eat? _____

Day 3

Use the line plot to answer the questions.

Sugar Used in Cookie Recipes (c.)

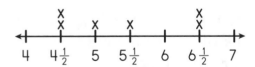

4    $4\frac{1}{2}$ 5 $5\frac{1}{2}$ 6 $6\frac{1}{2}$ 7

1. How many total cups of sugar were used in all of the cookies? _____

2. How many recipes called for $6\frac{1}{2}$ cups of sugar? _____

3. What is the difference between the greatest and least amounts of sugar used in the recipes? _____

Day 4

Draw all of the lines of symmetry.

1.

2.
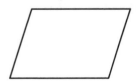

3.

---

1. Write <, >, or = to make the statement true.

$$\frac{2}{12} \bigcirc \frac{1}{2}$$

2. $\frac{5}{6}$
    $-\ \frac{1}{6}$
    _____

3. Decompose in two ways.

$$\frac{}{12} + \frac{}{12} = \frac{4}{12}$$

$$\frac{}{12} + \frac{}{12} = \frac{4}{12}$$

4. Elijah needs $\frac{6}{10}$ of a cup of pecans to make 1 pecan pie. If Elijah wants to make 4 pies, how many cups of pecans will he need?

_____

5. $3\frac{1}{8}$
    $-\ 2\frac{5}{8}$
    _____

6. Shannon washed $\frac{7}{15}$ of a bag of potatoes. She left the rest in a basket outside. How much of the bag did Shannon leave outside?

_____

7. How many total cups of flour were used in all of the cakes? _____

8. What is the difference between the greatest amount of flour used and the least amount of flour used? _____

Flour Used in Cakes (c.)

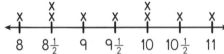

 Compare a bar graph to a line plot. How are they the same? How are they different? What is one situation you can think of where it would be better to use a bar graph than a line plot? Explain your reasoning.

Fluency Blast

Practice using mental math. Multiply each number by 4.

20   8   15   12   9   5   30   25   6   11   4   7

○○○○

Day 1

1. Write the decimal.

   $\dfrac{28}{100}$ = _____

2. $\begin{array}{r} \frac{9}{10} \\ -\ \frac{4}{10} \\ \hline \end{array}$

3. $\begin{array}{r} 12\frac{5}{12} \\ -\ 10\frac{7}{12} \\ \hline \end{array}$

4. $6 \times \dfrac{3}{10}$ = _____

5. Round **139,646** to the nearest ten.

   _____

Day 2

1. At a campsite, 65 campers arrive. There are 8 campers who go home early. If 9 campers sleep in one tent, how many tents do the campers need? _____

2. Complete the table.

	× 2
200	400
201	
202	
203	
204	

Day 3

Use the line plot to answer the questions.

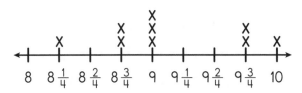

Miles Run

1. How many miles were run altogether?

   _____

2. How many times were the miles run 9 or greater? _____

3. What is the difference between the longest distance run and the shortest distance run?

   _____

Day 4

Identify each pair of lines as **parallel**, **intersecting**, or **perpendicular**.

1.

   _____

2.

   _____

3.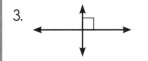

   _____

1. Write the decimal.

   $\dfrac{72}{100}$ _____

2. Renee ate $\dfrac{5}{12}$ of a banana. Camden ate $\dfrac{3}{12}$ of the same banana. How much more of the banana did Renee eat than Camden?

   _____

3.
$$6\dfrac{7}{10}$$
$$-\ 2\dfrac{3}{10}$$

4. $7 \times \dfrac{3}{10} =$ _____

5.
$$\dfrac{9}{8}$$
$$-\ \dfrac{1}{8}$$

6. Uri needs $\dfrac{1}{6}$ of a tablespoon of vanilla to make one milk shake. If Uri wants to make 8 milk shakes, how much vanilla will he need?

   _____

7. If you add all of the distances run, what is the total distance? _____

8. What is the difference between the longest and the shortest distance run? _____

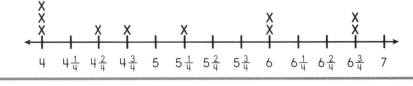

Kilometers Run

 In problem 6, Uri needs $\dfrac{1}{6}$ of a tablespoon of vanilla for one milk shake. He discovered that he also needed $\dfrac{1}{2}$ of a tablespoon of vanilla for every two scoops of ice cream. What information would Uri need to know to figure out how much vanilla to use in all?

Fluency Blast

Practice using mental math. Find the equivalent fractions.

$$\frac{1}{2} = \frac{}{36} = \frac{}{18} = \frac{}{16} = \frac{}{42} = \frac{}{48} = \frac{}{12} = \frac{}{24} = \frac{}{40}$$

○○○○

Day 1

1. Write <, >, or = to make the statement true.

$$\frac{2}{3} \bigcirc \frac{1}{2}$$

2. $$\begin{array}{r} \frac{7}{10} \\ - \frac{5}{10} \\ \hline \end{array}$$

3. If $\frac{7}{8} = 7 \times \left(\frac{1}{8}\right)$, then $\frac{6}{7} = \boxed{} \times \left(\frac{}{}\right)$.

4. $4 \times \frac{5}{8} =$ _____

5. $1{,}070 \div 2 =$ _____

Day 2

1. Corrina uses $\frac{2}{5}$ of a cup of sugar in each small cake. If she is making 9 small cakes, how much sugar does she use? _____

2. Complete the table.

+ 30	
820	850
830	
840	
850	
860	

Day 3

Write the value of each missing angle.

1. 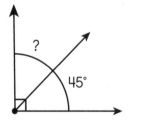 _____

2. 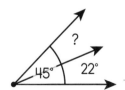 _____

3. 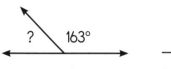 _____

Day 4

Identify each quadrilateral or triangle.

1.  _____

2. 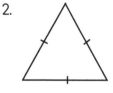 _____

3. 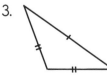 _____

1. $\dfrac{8}{8}$
    $-\dfrac{3}{8}$

2. $5\dfrac{1}{3} - 4\dfrac{2}{3} =$ _____

3. If $\dfrac{4}{9} = 4 \times \left(\dfrac{1}{9}\right)$, then $\dfrac{7}{11} = \boxed{} \times \left(\dfrac{}{}\right)$.

4. Taylor is using $\dfrac{1}{5}$ of a cup of barbecue sauce on each piece of chicken. If Taylor is making 8 pieces of chicken, how much barbecue sauce does he need? _____

5. Write <, >, or = to make the statement true.

    $\dfrac{1}{2}$ ◯ $\dfrac{4}{8}$

6. Write the decimal.

    $\dfrac{95}{100} =$ _____

7. Write the value of the missing angle.

    25°   ?

    _____

8. Name the shape.

    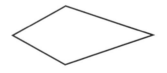

    _____

 In problem 4, Taylor needs more barbeque sauce for his chicken. His mom brought home 8 ounces of barbeque sauce to add to the 4 ounces they had at home. What steps will you take to figure out if Taylor has enough barbeque sauce?

   CD-104974 • © Carson-Dellosa

Fluency Blast

Practice using mental math. Find the equivalent fractions.

$$\frac{1}{3} = \frac{}{36} = \frac{}{18} = \frac{}{21} = \frac{}{42} = \frac{}{45} = \frac{}{12} = \frac{}{24} = \frac{}{33}$$

○○○○

Day 1

1. 89,876
   − 46,987
   _____

2. Rewrite in standard form.

   two hundred fifty-eight thousand six hundred eight

   _____

3. $\frac{}{10} = \frac{30}{100}$

4. Write the decimal. $\frac{73}{100}$ = _____

5. Write <, >, or = to make the statement true.

   0.45 ◯ 0.53

Day 2

1. Kenyon had $\frac{7}{8}$ of a bottle of water left. Ellen had $\frac{5}{8}$ of a bottle of water left. How much more water did Kenyon have left than Ellen?

   _____

2. The candy jar had 271 pieces of candy in it. Mia adds 41 pieces of candy to it. If the candy is divided equally between 8 people, how many pieces will each person get?

   _____

3. Lee ate $\frac{4}{6}$ of an apple pie. Chloe ate $\frac{1}{6}$ of the same apple pie. How much more apple pie did Lee eat than Chloe? _____

Day 3

Use a protractor to measure each angle.

1.

_____

2.
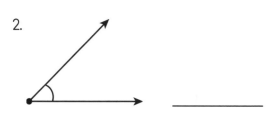
_____

3.
_____

Day 4

1. How many of each angle are in this shape?

   acute _____ obtuse _____ right _____

2. Name the angle.

   _____

3. Draw parallel lines.

1. Write <, >, or = to make the statement true.

    0.28 ◯ 0.28

2. $7 \times \frac{1}{3} =$ _____

3.
    $$\begin{array}{r} 9{,}896 \\ \times\ 8 \\ \hline \end{array}$$

4. Nick needed $\frac{7}{10}$ of a package of marbles for each gift bag. If he had to make 5 gift bags, how many packages of marbles did he need?

    _____

5. Round **354,145** to the nearest hundred thousand. _____

6. $\frac{9}{10} - \frac{3}{5} =$ _____

7. Use a protractor to measure the angle.

    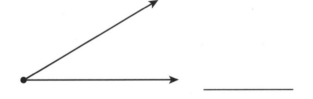

    _____

8. Name the triangle. Write both names.

    _____
    _____

 How do you identify parallel or perpendicular lines on paper? How do you identify them in the real world? How are the two the same and different?

Fluency Blast

Practice using mental math. Find the equivalent fractions.

$$\frac{1}{4} = \frac{}{36} = \frac{}{20} = \frac{}{16} = \frac{}{44} = \frac{}{48} = \frac{}{12} = \frac{}{24} = \frac{}{40}$$

○○○○

Day 1

1. $4 \times \dfrac{4}{9} =$ _____

2. $\dfrac{9}{10} + \dfrac{4}{100} =$ _____

3. $3{,}773 \div 7 =$ _____

4. $\begin{array}{r} 86{,}598 \\ -\ 43{,}786 \\ \hline \end{array}$

5. Round **539,245** to the nearest hundred thousand. _____

Day 2

1. Felipe spends 40 minutes caring for Mr. Murphy's dog. Then, he spends 25 minutes folding laundry. Next, he spends 25 minutes cleaning his room. How long does it take Felipe to do all of his chores? _____

2. Adrian, Casey, and Henry have a total of $26. Adrian has the most money. Casey has 2 times as much money as Henry. Adrian has $11. How much money does Casey have? _____

3. Erica packs 176 comic books in 8 different boxes. She packs an equal number of comic books in each box. How many comic books does she pack in each box? _____

Day 3

Write the value of each missing angle.

1.
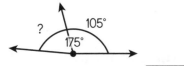

_____

2.
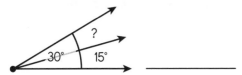

_____

3.

105°

_____

Day 4

1. How many of each angle are in this shape?

acute _____ obtuse _____ right _____

2. Draw perpendicular lines.

3. Name the shape.

_____

---

1. Derek wakes up at 9:20. It takes him 35 minutes to fold four loads of laundry, 30 minutes to bathe the dog, 55 minutes to bake brownies, and 1 hour to mow the lawn. Then, he gets to rest. What time does Derek get to rest? _____

2. $\frac{2}{5} + \frac{3}{4} =$ _____

3. $6\frac{2}{4} + 1\frac{3}{4} =$ _____

4. Dawson travels 18 kilometers total to and from school every day. How many kilometers does Dawson travel to and from school in 20 days?

   _____

5.
$$\begin{array}{r} 66{,}987 \\ -\ 56{,}987 \\ \hline \end{array}$$

6. $7{,}650 \div 8 =$ _____

7. Write the value of the missing angle.

   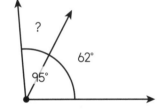

   _____

8. Name the triangle. Write both names.

   _____
   _____

 In problem 4, Dawson travels 18 kilometers to and from school every day. What information would you need to find out how long Dawson spent traveling? How would that change the way you solved the problem?

Fluency Blast

Practice using mental math. Find the equivalent fractions.

$\dfrac{2}{3} = \dfrac{}{12}$ $\dfrac{8}{9} = \dfrac{}{54}$ $\dfrac{1}{8} = \dfrac{}{32}$ $\dfrac{5}{9} = \dfrac{}{81}$ $\dfrac{2}{9} = \dfrac{}{18}$ $\dfrac{3}{4} = \dfrac{}{16}$

○○○○

Day 1

1. Round **856,755** to the nearest hundred thousand. _____

2. $\dfrac{5}{10} + \dfrac{2}{100} = \dfrac{}{100}$

3. Write the decimal.
   $\dfrac{31}{100} =$ _____

4. Decompose in two ways.

   $\dfrac{}{18} + \dfrac{}{18} = \dfrac{5}{18}$

   $\dfrac{}{18} + \dfrac{}{18} = \dfrac{5}{18}$

Day 2

1. Complete the table.

lb.	oz.
1	16
2	
3	
4	
5	

2. Kayla runs 153 kilometers over a 9-day period. It takes Kayla about 10 minutes to run each kilometer. If Kayla ran an equal number of kilometers each day, how many kilometers did Kayla run each day? _____

Day 3

Use a protractor to measure each angle.

1.
 _____

2.
_____

3.  _____

Day 4

1. Which word best describes this triangle?

   A. equilateral   B. isosceles   C. scalene

2. Draw intersecting lines that are not perpendicular.

3. Name the angle.

   _____

1. Ethan's Pizza Palace has 712 chairs. Each table has 4 chairs. How many tables are in the restaurant? _____

2. Complete the table.

kg	g
1	1,000
2	
3	
4	
5	

3. Round **78,232** to the nearest thousand.

_____

4. $2 \times \dfrac{3}{10} =$ _____

5. Decompose in two ways.

$$\dfrac{}{13} + \dfrac{}{13} = \dfrac{9}{13}$$

$$\dfrac{}{13} + \dfrac{}{13} = \dfrac{9}{13}$$

6. Delaney babysits 6 Saturdays in a row. Each Saturday, she earns $10.75. How much money does Delaney earn in all 6 Saturdays combined?

_____

7. Write the value of the missing angle.

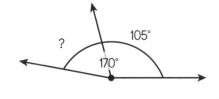

105°

?

170°

_____

8. Name the angle.

U

W

V

_____

 Look at problem 6. Delaney wants to figure out how much money she makes babysitting each hour. What information does she need? What steps could she take to calculate her hourly rate?

CD-104974 • © Carson-Dellosa

Fluency Blast

Practice using mental math. Find the equivalent fractions.

$\frac{2}{5} = \frac{}{10}$ $\frac{7}{8} = \frac{}{56}$ $\frac{2}{3} = \frac{}{15}$ $\frac{3}{4} = \frac{}{24}$ $\frac{3}{5} = \frac{}{15}$ $\frac{3}{7} = \frac{}{14}$

○○○○

Day 1

1. Write <, >, or = to make the statement true.

    0.72 ◯ 0.7

2. Round **65,367** to the nearest ten.

    _____

3.   23,496
    − 19,001
    _____

4. 1,764 ÷ 9 = _____

5. $4 \times \frac{5}{6} =$ _____

Day 2

1. Complete the table.

− 150	
1,278	1,128
1,288	
1,298	
1,308	
1,318	

2. Cole's milkshake recipe calls for $\frac{7}{10}$ of a scoop of ice cream. Ivy's recipe calls for $\frac{8}{9}$ of a scoop of ice cream. How much more ice cream is needed for Ivy's milkshake than Cole's?

    _____

Day 3

1. Draw an angle that is 30°.

2. Draw an angle that is 110°.

3. Write the value of the missing angle.

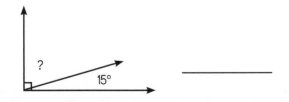

Day 4

1. Which word best describes this triangle?

    A. equilateral   B. isosceles   C. scalene

2. Name the type of angle.

 _____

3. Draw a triangle that has angle measurements of 60°, 60°, and 60°. What kind of triangle is it?

    _____

1. Complete the table.

+ 112	
901	1,013
921	
941	
961	
981	

2. Write <, >, or = to make the statement true.

0.49 ◯ 0.39

3. Harry has 18 marbles. His older brother has 7.5 times as many marbles as Harry. How many marbles does his older brother have?

_____

4. What kind of angle is shown?

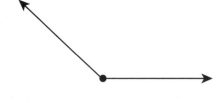

_____

5. Draw a right angle.

6. Carmon's Italian Restaurant put $\frac{1}{3}$ of a gallon of oil in one batch of salad dressing. How many gallons of oil would be used in 4 batches of salad dressing? _____

7. Use a protractor to measure the angle.

 _____

8. Draw a triangle that has angle measurements of 45°, 45°, and 90°. What kind of triangle is it? Write both names.

_____

_____

 Why do you think there are only three basic types of triangles? How many basic types of quadrilaterals are there? Make a chart to group the quadrilaterals based on different ways they are alike.

Fluency Blast

Practice using mental math. Find the equivalent fractions.

$\dfrac{1}{6} = \dfrac{}{12}$ $\dfrac{4}{6} = \dfrac{20}{}$ $\dfrac{3}{7} = \dfrac{}{21}$ $\dfrac{5}{6} = \dfrac{}{42}$ $\dfrac{2}{6} = \dfrac{}{36}$ $\dfrac{5}{8} = \dfrac{40}{}$

Day 1

1. Round **234,775** to the nearest hundred.

   _____

2. Rewrite in word form.

   560,654

   _____

   _____

3. If $\dfrac{1}{10} + \dfrac{6}{100} = \dfrac{16}{100}$, then $\dfrac{1}{10} + \dfrac{8}{100} = \dfrac{}{100}$.

4. Decompose $\dfrac{8}{15}$ in two ways.

Day 2

1. David needs 204 inches of yarn. How many yards should he buy? _____

2. Complete the table.

L	mL
1	1,000
2	
3	
4	
5	

Day 3

Draw angles for each measurement.

1. 50°

2. 125°

3. 70°

4. 45°

Day 4

1. Which word best describes this triangle?

   A. right B. acute C. obtuse

2. Draw a triangle that has angle measurements of 30°, 60°, and 90°. What kind of triangle is it?

   _____

3. Name the ray.

   _____

1. 30 liters = _____ milliliters

2. The toy train track is 90 inches long. How many feet long is the train track?

    _____

3. Emily bought some stamps that had flower, book, and flag designs. Emily bought 29 flower stamps. She bought 12 more book stamps than flower stamps and 20 fewer flag stamps than book stamps. How many stamps did she buy altogether? _____

4. Decompose $\frac{5}{6}$ in two ways.

5. If $\frac{2}{10} + \frac{2}{100} = \frac{22}{100}$, then $\frac{4}{10} + \frac{5}{100} = \frac{}{100}$.

6. A moving company is able to move 82 boxes every hour. How many boxes are they able to move during a 9-hour workday?

    _____

7. Draw a 170° angle.

8. Name the segment.

    _____

Draw three different quadrilaterals. Measure all of the angles in one quadrilateral and then add all of the angle measurements. Repeat with the other quadrilaterals. What prediction can you make about the angle sums in quadrilaterals?

Fluency Blast

Practice using mental math. Find the equivalent decimals.

$$\frac{2}{10} \qquad \frac{9}{10} \qquad \frac{8}{10} \qquad \frac{5}{10} \qquad \frac{4}{10} \qquad \frac{3}{10} \qquad \frac{88}{100} \qquad \frac{52}{100} \qquad \frac{25}{100} \qquad \frac{55}{100} \qquad \frac{30}{100} \qquad \frac{14}{100}$$

○○○○

Day 1

1. 19,077
    + 12,465

2. $3\frac{1}{4} + 3\frac{5}{8} =$ _____

3. $56 \times 22 =$ _____

    $692 \div 4 =$ _____

4. Decompose $\frac{7}{11}$ in two ways.

Day 2

1. Clarke has 360 marbles in bags. If 9 marbles are in each bag, how many bags does Clarke have? _____

    How many bags will he have if he gives 14 bags to his brother? _____

2. Melinda picked 54 daisies. Keisha picked 1.5 times more daisies than Melinda. How many daisies did Keisha pick? _____

3. The white horse ran $2\frac{1}{5}$ miles. The spotted horse ran $1\frac{2}{3}$ miles. How many total miles did the horses run? _____

Day 3

Use what you know about right and straight angles to find each missing angle measure.

1.
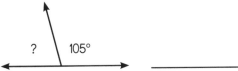
_____

2.
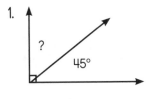
_____

3.
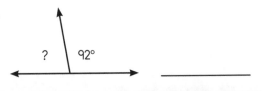
_____

Day 4

1. Which word best describes this triangle?

    A. right   B. acute   C. obtuse

2. Name the line.

    _____

Name _____

1. Decompose $\frac{10}{11}$ in two ways.

2. Paul bought 87 cases of water for his restaurant. Each case had 24 bottles of water in it. How many bottles of water did Paul buy in all?

   _____

3. $683 \times 3 =$ _____

   $1,194 \div 6 =$ _____

4. $\begin{array}{r} 87,662 \\ -\ 59,889 \\ \hline \end{array}$

5. $\frac{1}{7} + 1\frac{4}{9} =$ _____

6. $\begin{array}{r} 15,597 \\ +\ 2,504 \\ \hline \end{array}$

7. Find the missing angle.

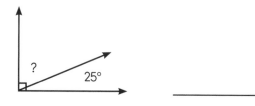

   _____

8. Name the line.

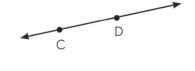

   _____

 Draw a diagram of your classroom from the top down. Label the points, the lines, and the angles. Are there any parallel or perpendicular lines? What else would you need to know for your diagram?

CD-104974 • © Carson-Dellosa

Fluency Blast

Practice using mental math. Find the equivalent fraction for each decimal.

0.5   0.9   0.7   0.6   0.8   0.4   0.62   0.58   0.22   0.36   0.25   0.78

○○○○○

Day 1

1. $3\frac{5}{8}$

    $+\quad\frac{7}{8}$

2. Write <, >, or = to make the statement true.

    $\frac{1}{5}\bigcirc\frac{3}{10}$

3. Rewrite in standard form.

    eighty-nine thousand nine hundred eighty

    _____

4. Decompose $\frac{6}{15}$ in two ways.

Day 2

1. Determine the 12th shape of the pattern.

    _____

2. Claire orders 5 boxes of toothbrushes. If she has 765 toothbrushes in all, how many are in each box? _____

3. Veronica saw 142 tourists in July, August, and September. She saw 35 tourists in July and 89 tourists in August. How many tourists did Veronica see in September? _____

Day 3

1. What is the value of the complete angle?

    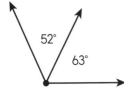

    52°

    63°   _____

    Use a protractor to measure each angle.

2. _____

3. _____

Day 4

1. Brantley drew a shape. The shape had 3 unequal angles. What shape could Brantley have drawn? _____

2. Name the segment.

    K
    J

    _____

3. Draw an irregular hexagon.

1.

$11\frac{1}{4}$

$+ \ 2\frac{3}{4}$
___

2. Round **15,454** to the nearest thousand.

___

3. Write <, >, or = to make the statement true.

$\frac{3}{12} \bigcirc \frac{1}{3}$

4. If $\frac{6}{10} + \frac{5}{100} = \frac{65}{100}$, then $\frac{5}{10} + \frac{9}{100} = \frac{\ }{100}$.

5. Write the decimal.

$\frac{7}{100} =$ ___

6. $\frac{5}{10} = \frac{\ }{100}$

7. What is the complete value of the angle?

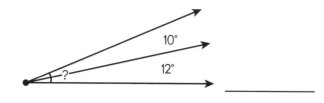

___

8. Name the ray.

___

 Prove that a line is 180°.

Fluency Blast

Practice using mental math. Find the simplest form for each fraction.

$\dfrac{6}{8}$ $\dfrac{3}{24}$ $\dfrac{20}{35}$ $\dfrac{15}{20}$ $\dfrac{10}{20}$ $\dfrac{6}{16}$ $\dfrac{5}{20}$ $\dfrac{4}{8}$ $\dfrac{4}{16}$ $\dfrac{6}{9}$ $\dfrac{4}{20}$ $\dfrac{3}{15}$

○○○○

Day 1

1. $\dfrac{2}{11} + \dfrac{5}{11} =$ _____

2. $\begin{array}{r} 56,847 \\ -45,096 \\ \hline \end{array}$ 3. $\begin{array}{r} 56,897 \\ -45,696 \\ \hline \end{array}$

4. Write <, >, or = to make the statement true.

$\dfrac{3}{5}$ ◯ $\dfrac{1}{2}$

5. Write the decimal.

$\dfrac{45}{100} =$ _____

Day 2

1. Ryan eats $\dfrac{5}{10}$ of a sandwich. Amy eats $\dfrac{3}{10}$ of the same sandwich. How much more of the sandwich did Ryan eat than Amy?

_____

2. Whitney has 13 stickers. Arianna has 6 times as many stickers as Whitney. How many stickers does Arianna have? _____

3. Baily has 109 gems. Ronnie has 3 times as many gems as Baily. How many gems does Ronnie have? _____

Day 3

1. Use a protractor to measure the angle.

_____

2. What is the value of the complete angle?

45°

97°

_____

3. Draw an angle with a value of 65°.

Day 4

Use the figure to answer the questions.

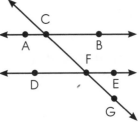

1. Name four points. _____, _____,

_____, _____

2. Name two parallel lines. _____,

_____

3. Name two intersecting lines. _____,

_____

4. Name three rays. _____,

_____, _____

1. Write <, >, or = to make the statement true.

$$\frac{1}{3} \bigcirc \frac{1}{5}$$

2.   25,934
    + 18,507

3. $5 \times \frac{2}{3} =$ _____

4. $\frac{5}{8}$
     $- \frac{1}{8}$

5. Britney needs $\frac{5}{8}$ of a cup of oatmeal for each batch of cookies she is baking. If she wants to bake 3 batches of cookies, how much oatmeal will she need? _____

6. Thad has 294 marshmallows. He drops 16. If 10 people share the remaining marshmallows, how many will each person get?

_____

7. Draw an angle with a value of 115°.

8. Draw ray *AB*.

Explain how to use a protractor to draw an angle.

Fluency Blast

Practice using mental math. Find the simplest form for each fraction.

$\frac{3}{12}$ $\frac{5}{15}$ $\frac{8}{16}$ $\frac{7}{21}$ $\frac{5}{25}$ $\frac{15}{30}$ $\frac{2}{8}$ $\frac{14}{21}$ $\frac{12}{16}$ $\frac{4}{8}$ $\frac{7}{14}$ $\frac{20}{30}$

Day 1

1. $\frac{7}{8}$
    $-\frac{2}{12}$
    _____

2. $3 \times \frac{1}{4} =$

3. $\frac{5}{10} + \frac{7}{100} = \frac{}{100}$

4. Write the decimal.
    $\frac{6}{10} =$ _____

5. Round **138,206** to the nearest ten thousand.
    _____

Day 2

1. Samaria needs $\frac{1}{4}$ of a gallon of water for her water balloon. Norris needs $\frac{3}{8}$ of a gallon of water for his water balloon. How much more water does Norris need than Samaria?

    _____

2. Complete the table.

	× 3
41	123
45	
49	
53	
56	

Day 3

1. Use a protractor to measure the angle.

    _____

2. What is the value of the complete angle?

    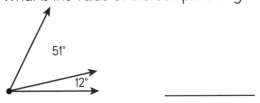
    51°
    12°
    _____

3. Draw an angle with a value of 56°.

Day 4

Use the figure to answer the questions.

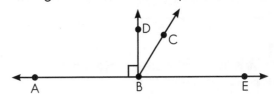

1. Name 3 three points. _____,
    _____, _____

2. Name two perpendicular lines. _____,
    _____

3. Name four line segments. _____,
    _____, _____, _____

4. Name four rays. _____, _____,
    _____, _____

---

1. $8 \times \dfrac{2}{6} =$ _____

2. Write the decimal.

   $\dfrac{33}{100} =$ _____

3. $\dfrac{6}{10} + \dfrac{3}{100} = \dfrac{}{100}$

4. $\begin{array}{r} 12\dfrac{7}{9} \\ - \ 10\dfrac{3}{12} \\ \hline \end{array}$

5. Tisha went out to eat with her friends on Monday, Tuesday, and Wednesday. She spent $5.60 on Monday, $8.50 on Tuesday, and $10.75 on Wednesday. How much more money did Tisha spend on Monday and Tuesday combined than she spent on Wednesday?

   _____

6. Mandy is 6 years old. Her mom is 5.5 times as old as Mandy is. How old is Mandy's mom?

   _____

7. What is the value of the complete angle?

   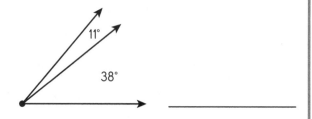

   11°

   38°

   _____

8. Draw line segment *RS*.

 What strategies help you to solve word problems? Which ones are your favorites? Why?

CD-104974 • © Carson-Dellosa

Fluency Blast

Practice using mental math. Find the simplest form for each fraction.

$\dfrac{4}{12}$ $\dfrac{2}{8}$ $\dfrac{5}{30}$ $\dfrac{3}{9}$ $\dfrac{2}{6}$ $\dfrac{3}{15}$ $\dfrac{3}{12}$ $\dfrac{8}{24}$ $\dfrac{6}{18}$ $\dfrac{15}{21}$ $\dfrac{7}{28}$ $\dfrac{12}{15}$

○○○○

Day 1

1.
$$4\tfrac{2}{8}$$
$$+\ 1\tfrac{7}{8}$$

2.
$$5\tfrac{1}{6}$$
$$-\ 3\tfrac{4}{6}$$

3. Write the decimal.

$\dfrac{65}{100} =$ _____

4. Write <, >, or = to make the statement true.

$$\dfrac{4}{10} \bigcirc \dfrac{1}{8}$$

5. $\dfrac{}{10} = \dfrac{60}{100}$

Day 2

1. Joshua saves $2,854. He wants to invest half of the money and put the rest in his savings account. How much money will Joshua invest?

_____

2. Sarah got 10 marbles from the store and 5 from her mom. Sarah's teacher gave her 18 marbles. Sarah gave 12 marbles to her friend. How many marbles does Sarah have left?

_____

3. Lamonte needs 16 quarts of punch for a party. How many gallons of punch does Lamonte need to buy? _____

Day 3

1. Write the value of the angle.

_____

2. What is the value of the missing angle?

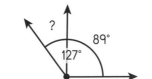

_____

3. What is the value of the complete angle?

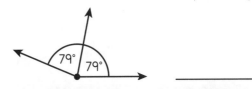

_____

Day 4

Determine if the shape has one or more lines of symmetry and write **yes** or **no**. If yes, draw all of the lines of symmetry.

1. _____

2.  _____

3. _____

4. _____

---

1. Melanie put $582 in the bank. Her brother put 3 times as much money in the bank. Her sister put $\frac{1}{3}$ as much money in the bank. How much money combined did Melanie's brother and sister put in the bank? _____

2.
$$1\frac{2}{6}$$
$$+ \ 1\frac{5}{8}$$
_____

3.
$$\frac{11}{12}$$
$$- \ \frac{6}{10}$$
_____

4. Marcella sold pizzas yesterday. Of the pizzas she sold, $\frac{1}{6}$ were small, $\frac{1}{3}$ were large, and $\frac{1}{2}$ were extra large. What fraction of the pizzas sold were large or extra large?

_____

5. $4,963 \div 7 =$ _____

6. Two boxes of gold weigh 4 pounds 8 ounces each. Each pound is worth $500. How much are the boxes of gold worth altogether?

_____

7. Use a protractor to measure the angle.

_____

8. Determine if the shape has one or more lines of symmetry and write **yes** or **no**. If yes, draw all of the lines of symmetry.

_____

 Design a classroom that has at least two lines of symmetry. What were some things that made this task easy? What were some things that made this task difficult?

CD-104974 • © Carson-Dellosa

Answer Key

Page 9
Fluency Blast: 19, 57, 48, 19, 34, 32, 67, 92, 51, 16, 29, 39; **Day 1:** 1. 648; 2. 2,191; 3. 100,087; 4. 300, 500, 700, 800; **Day 2:** 1. 31,033 points; 2. 20, 30, 40, 50; **Day 3:** 1. 4:15; 2. 20 students; 3. 10; **Day 4:** 1. $\overleftrightarrow{MN}$; 2. $\overrightarrow{XY}$; 3. Check students' work.

Page 10
1. 500, 200, 200; 2. 4,068; 3. 59,006; 4. 18, 27, 36, 45; 5. $34,424; 6. 16, 18, 20; 7. 120; 8. angle PQR

Page 11
Fluency Blast: 13, 16, 13, 35, 37, 39, 11, 12, 15, 79, 11, 57; **Day 1:** 1. 129; 2. $1.06; 3. 14,648; 4. 50,000; 5. >; **Day 2:** 1. 7, 12, 20, 24; 2. 154 people; **Day 3:** 1. C; 2. 5:45; 3. 12,320; 4. 200; **Day 4:** 1. perpendicular; 2. parallel; 3. intersecting

Page 12
1. square; 2. 9,710; 3. 65,305; 4. 44,000; 5. $9,007; 6. 67, 57, 62, 55; 7. 3:45; 8. 10

Page 13
Fluency Blast: 55, 43, 38, 61, 70, 9, 5, 12, 31, 78, 84, 23; **Day 1:** 1. 3 × 4 = 12; 2. 65,365; 3. 110; 4. 1, 2, 4, 8, composite; **Day 2:** 1. 120, 121, 122, 123; 2. 201 pages; **Day 3:** 1. 15; 2. 10; 3. 88; 4. 160; 5. 8; **Day 4:** 1. acute; 2. right; 3. obtuse

Page 14
1. 55,463; 2. 45,400; 3. 1, 3, 9, composite; 4. 521, 546, 571, 596; 5. 2 × 3 = 6; 6. 20 photos; 7. 160; 8. 108

Page 15
Fluency Blast: 12, 10, 64, 36, 27, 8, 0, 9, 24, 10, 50, 49; **Day 1:** 1. 1,597,772; 2. 180,000; 3. 7,661; 4. 57; **Day 2:** 1. 1, 11, prime; 2. 60, 90, 120; 3. 22 buds; **Day 3:** 1. 200, 300, 400, 500; 2. 300 L; **Day 4:** 1. acute; 2. right; 3. obtuse

Page 16
1. $9; 2. 283; 3. 100; 4. 75,317; 5. 81,300; 6. 10,000; 7. 43 acorns; 8. acute

Page 17
Fluency Blast: 6, 7, 16, 48, 35, 0, 18, 30, 54, 24, 60, 0; **Day 1:** 1. 100; 2. 31,932; 3. 73,859; 4. 900,000; 5. >; **Day 2:** 1. triangle; 2. 60 arms; 3. 8, 11, 6, 10; 4. 12, 15, 18, 21, 24; **Day 3:** 1. 4; 2. 5,280; 3. 6; 4. 9; 5. 8; **Day 4:** 1. $\overrightarrow{QP}$, $\overrightarrow{QR}$; 2. Q; 3. angle PQR

Page 18
1. 10; 2. 10,251; 3. 2,067; 4. hexagon; 5. 87,000; 6. 45, 63, 36; 7. 2,160; 8. 190,687

Page 19
Fluency Blast: 24, 21, 80, 36, 15, 63, 10, 32, 25, 30, 4, 6; **Day 1:** 1. 359,006; 2. <; 3. 300; 4. 12,120; 5. no; **Day 2:** 1. circle; 2. 72 mi.; 3. 1, 19, prime; 4. 58 books; **Day 3:** 1. 3,300; 2. 14,000; 3. 47,000; 4. 9; **Day 4:** 1–2. Check students' work. 3. parallel lines

Page 20
1. 906,192; 2. 599; 3. 41,984; 4. 713,900; 5. 1, 2, 3, 5, 6, 10, 15, 30, composite; 6. dark circle; 7. 1,500; 8. obtuse

Page 21
Fluency Blast: 4, 36, 21, 45, 42, 12, 0, 54, 2, 24, 100, 0; **Day 1:** 1. 41,890; 2. 926; 3. 408,503; 4. yes; 5. >; **Day 2:** 1, 3, 13, 39, composite; 2. 585, 575, 565, 555, 545; 3. 7 marbles; 4. 88 legs; **Day 3:** 1. 9:10; 2. 7 1/4 in.; 3. 5,000; 4. 840; **Day 4:** 1. perpendicular; 2. Check students' work. 3. B

Page 22
1. 8 pencils; 2. 1, 17, prime; 3. 1/4; 4. >; 5. 4,609; 6. 9 1/2 in.; 7. 10:20; 8. 8,000

Page 23
Fluency Blast: 52, 204, 270, 376, 747, 343, 468, 516, 576, 96, 174, 210; **Day 1:** 1. 64; 2. 3 × 5; 3. <; 4. 65,507; 5. 9,097; **Day 2:** 1, 2, 7, 14, composite; 2. 12, 15, 18, 21; **Day 3:** 1. 79,000 mL; 2. 4 L; 3. 50; **Day 4:** 1–2. Check students' work. 3. A

Answer Key

Page 24
1. 9, 11, 13, 15; 2. 1, 2, 3, 4, 6, 8, 12, 24, composite; 3. 594,026; 4. 212, 215, 218, 221, 224; 5. 100; 6. 112,539; 7. 70 L; 8. straight

Page 25
Fluency Blast: 378, 140, 88, 39, 77, 88, 252, 72, 416, 240, 273, 342; **Day 1:** 1. 633,795; 2. 209; 3. <; 4. 95,175; 5. 6 × 9 = 54; **Day 2:** 1. 1, 2, 3, 4, 6, 9, 12, 18, 36, composite; 2. dark circle; 3. $27; 4. 12 golf clubs; **Day 3:** 1. 9; 2. 60; 3. 110; 4. 7,000; 5. 40; **Day 4:** 1. rectangle; 2. trapezoid; 3. parallelogram; 4. rhombus

Page 26
1. $950; 2. 1, 23, prime; 3. 2,000 + 100 + 20 + 4; 4. 1,344; 5. 18 buckets; 6. =; 7. heart; 8. 23,000

Page 27
Fluency Blast: 114, 161, 213, 469, 152, 153, 576, 290, 378, 360, 108, 104; **Day 1:** 1. <; 2. 585,856, 1,074; 3. 87,478; 4. 999; **Day 2:** 1. 1, 2, 4, 5, 10, 20, composite; 2. 32 spots; 3. 29, 37, 46, 56; **Day 3:** 1. D; 2. 5:38; 3. 9; 4. 10; **Day 4:** 1. yes, Check students' work. 2. Check students' work. 3. B

Page 28
1. 1, 3, 11, 33, composite; 2. 77, 73, 69, 65, 61; 3. 17 stickers; 4. 200,000 + 50,000 + 9,000 + 300 + 40 + 1; 5. 55,451; 6. 13,000; 7. A; 8. 13,000

Page 29
Fluency Blast: 504, 136, 475, 180, 180, 171, 128, 156, 246, 608, 265, 819; **Day 1:** 1. 37,590; 2. 92,631; 3. 18,000; 4. >; 5. 7, 4, 5; **Day 2:** 1. 12 years old; 2. 110, 120, 130, 140; **Day 3:** 1. 225 yd.; 2. 14 m; 3. 42 km; **Day 4:** 1. isosceles; 2. scalene; 3. scalene; 4. equilateral

Page 30
1. 175 books; 2. 630,000; 3. 8; 4. 30, 35, 40, 45; 5. 24 hair bows; 6. Check students' work. 7. 35 cm; 8. 34 photos

Page 31
Fluency Blast: 48, 66, 432, 225, 588, 490, 86, 280, 66, 440, 146, 336; **Day 1:** 1. 827,672; 2. 273; 3. 435; 4. 125,199; 5. 601; **Day 2:** 1. $300; 2. 195 students; 3. 79, 72, 64, 55, 45; **Day 3:** 1. 24 ft.; 2. 22 in.; 3. 180 sq. in.; **Day 4:** 1. angle *BCD*, acute; 2. angle *QRS*, right; 3. angle *XYZ*, obtuse; 4. angle *PQR*, obtuse

Page 32
1. 104 people; 2. 621; 3. 376; 4. 195 animal crackers; 5. 65 in.; 6. 36 cm; 7. 288 times; 8. 144 mm

Page 33
Fluency Blast: 64, 90, 88, 36, 99, 100, 75, 66, 90, 30, 39, 48; **Day 1:** 1. 51; 2. 17,934; 3. 465,276; 4. 763; 5. 928; **Day 2:** 1. 1, 59, prime; 2. 282 light bulbs; 3. 17 in.; **Day 3:** 1. 62 ft.; 2. 9 in.; 3. 28 sq. in.; **Day 4:** Check students' work.

Page 34
1. 2,345; 2. 47 in.; 3. 33 cm; 4. 92; 5. 210 min.; 6. 39 in.; 7. 1,140 min.; 8. 96 mi.

Page 35
Fluency Blast: 5, 3, 6, 8, 8, 8, 4, 2, 5, 9; **Day 1:** 1. 2,322; 2. 282; 3. 36; 4. 28,989; 5. 217; **Day 2:** 1. 20, 24, 28, 32; 2. 4,428 people; **Day 3:** 1. 6 ft.; 2. 4 ft.; 3. 31 m; **Day 4:** Check students' work.

Page 36
1. 144 blueberries; 2. 7,029; 3. 1,152 people; 4. 8 ft.; 5. 22, 32, 42, 52; 6. 120 biscuits; 7. 8 ft.; 8. Check students' work.

Page 37
Fluency Blast: 7, 9, 6, 8, 9, 6, 10, 8, 6, 4; **Day 1:** 1. 234,608; 2. 513,667; 3. 129; 4. 9,892; 5. 268,700; **Day 2:** 1. $183; 2. 993, 994, 995, 996; 3. 1, 2, 4, 17, 34, 68, composite; **Day 3:** 1. 180 m; 2. 54 in.; 3. 48 mm; **Day 4:** Check students' work.

CD-104974 • © Carson-Dellosa

Answer Key

Page 38
1. 33,712; 2. 342,608; 3. 106,496; 4. 1, 67, prime;
5. 56 hr.; 6. 2,187 tickets; 7. 70 yd.; 8. 4 sets

Page 39
Fluency Blast: 7, 8, 5, 8, 5, 7, 5, 3, 5, 10;
Day 1: 334,614; 2. 98,081; 3. 1,564, 35; 4. fifty
thousand three hundred twenty-eight; 5. 462,150;
Day 2: 1. 1,656 ribbons; 2. 108, 111, 114, 117;
Day 3: 1. 10 yd.; 2. 6 cm; 3. Check students' work.
Day 4: Check students' work.

Page 40
1. 95,525; 2. 13r1; 3. five hundred five thousand two
hundred five; 4. $63; 5. 256 stickers; 6. 11,000;
7. 5 ft.; 8. Check students' work.

Page 41
Fluency Blast: 7, 4, 9, 6, 5, 7, 9, 6, 6, 10;
Day 1: 821,904; 2. 300,000; 3. 331,506; 4. <;
5. 8,008, 501; **Day 2:** 1. 52 people; 2. hexagon;
3. 1, 3, 5, 15, 25, 75, composite; **Day 3:** 1. 28 sq. in.;
2. 180 sq. in.; 3. 80 sq. km; **Day 4:** Check
students' work.

Page 42
1. 2,456; 2. 740,000; 3. 105,563; 4. 75 tickets;
5. 4,482 ft.; 6. 27 ft.; 7. 225 sq. mm; 8. Check
students' work.

Page 43
Fluency Blast: 5, 6, 7, 9, 8, 2, 6, 9, 8, 5;
Day 1: 1. 860,915; 2. 876,319; 3. 268,000; 4. <;
5. 2,024, 44 r4; **Day 2:** 1. 936 footballs; 2. 52, 56, 60,
64; **Day 3:** 1. 14 in.; 2. 24 in.; 3. 8 in.; **Day 4:** Check
students' work.

Page 44
1. 75,050; 2. 329,200; 3. 43,016; 4. 1,584 snowboards;
5. 520 mi.; 6. 192; 7. 9 ft.; 8. Check students' work.

Page 45
Fluency Blast: 392, 156, 102, 85, 175, 6, 7, 4, 6, 9;
Day 1: 1. 789; 2. 241,560; 3. eight hundred forty-one
thousand five hundred four; 4. 3,675, 950;
5. 1,526, 347; **Day 2:** 1. 18 ft.; 2. 56, 63, 70, 77;
Day 3: 1. 24 ft.; 2. 28 cm; 3. 280 m; **Day 4:** Check
students' work.

Page 46
1. $74; 2. 920, 930; 3. 28,688; 4. 7 ft.; 5. 460,000;
6. 922,107; 7. 310 in.; 8. Check students' work.

Page 47
Fluency Blast: 4, 7, 8, 28, 16, 630, 168, 135, 165, 133;
Day 1: 1. 870, 2,160; 2. 2,500; 3. 994,259; 4. <; 5. 23;
Day 2: 1. 30 baseball cards; 2. 167, 168, 169, 170;
Day 3: 1. 20 cm; 2. 70 sq. m; 3. 20 sq. m;
Day 4: Check students' work.

Page 48
1. $10; 2. 1,386, 10; 3. 608,900; 4. 8 in.; 5. 112 crafts;
6. >; 7. 208 cm; 8. Check students' work.

Page 49
Fluency Blast: (left to right) 8,000, 300, 90,000,
40,000, 500,000, 700, 1,000, 40, 5,000, 80,000;
Day 1: 1. 4/5; 2. 40; 3. 5 2/3; 4. 0.5; **Day 2:** 1. 25, 30,
35, 40; 2. 1 hr., 1/2 hr.; **Day 3:** 1. 19 books; 2. 2 in.;
3. 12 books; **Day 4:** 1. yes; 2. no; 3. yes

Page 50
1. 2/3; 2. 50; 3. 1 hr.; 4. 0.8; 5. 4 3/5; 6. 64 tickets;
7. no, no; 8. Check students' work.

Page 51
Fluency Blast: (left to right) 400, 7, 2,000, 9,000,
10,000, 20, 7,000, 900, 4,000, 60,000; **Day 1:** 1. <;
2. 1/2; 3. 540,000; 4. 80; 5. 77; **Day 2:** 1. 56 m;
2. 3/6 or 7/12 mi.; 16 m; **Day 3:** 1. 8 recipes;
2. 2 recipes; **Day 4:** 1. symmetrical;
2. nonsymmetrical; 3. symmetrical, Check students'
work.

Answer Key

Page 52

1. >; 2. 0.87; 3. 687,160; 4. 9/10 mi.; 5. 6 1/5; 6. 90;
7. 48; 8. nonsymmetrical

Page 53

Fluency Blast: (left to right) 600,000, 7,000,000,
80,000, 200,000, 34,000, 45,000, 5,200, 400,
10,000,000, 28,000,000; **Day 1:** 1. 4,5; 2. 5/12; 3.
0.49; 4. 60; 5. 83; **Day 2:** 1. 85 candy bars; 2. 1, 2,
4, 8, 16, composite; 3. 3/4 of a cup; **Day 3:** 1. 22
ribbons; 2. 2 in.; 3. 3 ribbons;
Day 4: 1–2. Check students' work.

Page 54

1. 1, 2, 17, 34, composite; 2. 70; 3. 0.64; 4. 1 1/4 of
a cup; 5. 1/2; 6. 24 years old; 7. Check students'
work. 8. 8 ribbons

Page 55

Fluency Blast: (left to right) 6,000, 400, 70,000,
50, 2,800, 7,900, 524, 58,200, 3,600, 90,000;
Day 1: 1. 0.14; 2. 16; 3. =; 4. 3 4/5; 5. 301, 651;
Day 2: 1. 5/6 of a pizza; 2. 9 ft.; 3. 75 key chains;
Day 3: 1. sunny; 2. 12 days; 3. cloudy;
Day 4: 1–2. Check students' work.

Page 56

1. 1 5/12 of a pizza; 2. 0.32; 3. =; 4. 36; 5. 408, 5,256;
6. 6 1/3; 7. Check students' work. 8. 2 days

Page 57

Fluency Blast: (left to right) 350, 36,000, 600,000,
20,000, 90,000, 2,400, 450,000, 540,000, 180,000,
2,500; **Day 1:** 1. 0.54; 2. 99/100; 3. 5 3/4; 4. 320,150;
5. 2/3; **Day 2:** 1. 3,882 flags; 2. 9/10 of the pie;
3. 132 lb.; **Day 3:** 1. 2 trees; 2. October; 3. 62 trees;
Day 4: 1–2. Check students' work.

Page 58

1. 7/12 of the bag; 2. 8; 3. 8 1/3; 4. 0.26; 5. 7/8;
6. 45 books, 90 books; 7. Check students' work.
8. 6 trees

Page 59

Fluency Blast: (left to right) 50, 20, 3,000, 10, 1,000,
10, 50, 1,000, 45, 2,000; **Day 1:** 1. 1/4; 2. 2 2/3;
3. 0.06; 4. 25; 5. 5, 1, 6; **Day 2:** 1. 1, 2, 3, 5, 6, 9, 10, 15,
18, 30, 45, 90, composite; 2. 12 ft.; 3. 5 1/3 lb.;
Day 3: 1. 14 pieces; 2. 4 pieces; 3. 1 1/4 in.;
Day 4: 1–3. Check students' work.

Page 60

1. 3 3/5 cups; 2. 9; 3. 6, 1, 10; 4. 1 3/5; 5. 1/3;
6. 3/8 of a pan; 7. 16 pieces; 8. 1 3/4 in.

Page 61

Fluency Blast: 40, 36, 30, 24, 38, 70, 60, 50, 32, 22,
48, 34; **Day 1:** 1. 0.68; 2. 3 2/5; 3. 1/6; 4. 2, 1, 8;
5. 1 1/5; **Day 2:** 1. 1/2 of the apple; 2. 43 paper clips,
7 paper clips; 3. 2/3 of a pizza; **Day 3:** 1. 18 sticks;
2. 3 sticks; 3. 7/8 in.; **Day 4:** 1–3. Check
students' work.

Page 62

1. 30; 2. 1 2/5; 3. 2 2/3 cups; 4. 9/10; 5. 0.29; 6. 2, 1, 4;
7. 9 7/8 in.; 8. 15 sticks

Page 63

Fluency Blast: 60, 24, 45, 36, 27, 15, 90, 75, 18, 33,
12, 21; **Day 1:** 1. 2, 7, 3, 6; 2. <; 3. 3 2/5; 4. 1/6; **Day 2:**
1. 20, 24, 28, 32; 2. 3/8 of the orange;
Day 3: 1. 32 1/2 cups; 2. 2 recipes; 3. 2 cups;
Day 4: 1–3. Check students' work.

Page 64

1. <; 2. 2/3; 3. 3, 1, 2, 2; 4. 2 2/5 cups; 5. 1/2;
6. 8/15 of the bag; 7. 85 cups; 8. 3 cups

Page 65

Fluency Blast: 80, 32, 60, 48, 36, 20, 120, 100, 24,
44, 16, 28; **Day 1:** 1. 0.28; 2. 1/2; 3. 1 5/6;
4. 1 4/5; 5. 139,650; **Day 2:** 1. 7 tents; 2. 402, 404,
406, 408; **Day 3:** 1. 82 1/4 mi.; 2. 6 times; 3. 1 3/4 mi.;
Day 4: 1. intersecting; 2. parallel; 3. perpendicular

CD-104974 • © Carson-Dellosa

Answer Key

Page 66
1. 0.72; 2. 1/6 of the banana; 3. 4 2/5; 4. 2 1/10;
5. 7/8; 6. 1 1/3 tbsp.; 7. 52 km; 8. 2 3/4 km

Page 67
Fluency Blast: 18, 9, 8, 21, 24, 6, 12, 20; **Day 1:** 1. >;
2. 1/5; 3. 6, 1, 7; 4. 2 1/2; 5. 535; **Day 2:** 1. 3 3/5 cups;
2. 860, 870, 880, 890; **Day 3:** 1. 45°; 2. 23°; 3. 17°;
Day 4: 1. parallelogram; 2. equilateral;
3. isoceles

Page 68
1. 5/8; 2. 2/3; 3. 7, 1, 11; 4. 1 3/5 cups; 5. =; 6. 0.95;
7. 155°; 8. kite

Page 69
Fluency Blast: 12, 6, 7, 14, 15, 4, 8, 11; **Day 1:** 1. 42,889;
2. 258,608; 3. 3; 4. 0.73; 5. <; **Day 2:** 1. 1/4 of a
bottle; 2. 39 pieces; 3. 1/2 of the pie; **Day 3:** 1. 90°;
2. 45°; 3. 173°; **Day 4:** 1. 2, 2, 0; 2. angle *XYZ*;
3. Check students' work.

Page 70
1. =; 2. 2 1/3; 3. 79,168; 4. 3 1/2 packages; 5. 400,000;
6. 3/10; 7. 30°; 8. isoceles, right

Page 71
Fluency Blast: 9, 5, 4, 11, 12, 3, 6, 10; **Day 1:** 1. 1 7/9;
2. 94/100; 3. 539; 4. 42,812; 5. 500,000;
Day 2: 1. 1 1/2 hr.; 2. $10; 3. 22 comic books;
Day 3: 1. 70°; 2. 15°; 3. 13°; **Day 4:** 1. 2, 0, 1; 2. Check
students' work. 3. pentagon

Page 72
1. 12:20; 2. 1 3/20; 3. 8 1/4; 4. 360 km; 5. 10,000;
6. 956r2; 7. 33°; 8. right, scalene

Page 73
Fluency Blast: 8, 48, 4, 45, 4, 12; **Day 1:** 1. 900,000;
2. 52; 3. 0.31; 4. Check students' work. **Day 2:** 1. 32,
48, 64, 80; 2. 17 km; **Day 3:** 1. 105°; 2. 95°; 3. 175°;
Day 4: 1. C; 2. Check students' work. 3. angle *LMN*

Page 74
1. 178 tables; 2. 2,000, 3,000, 4,000, 5,000;
3. 78,000; 4. 3/5; 5. Check students' work.
6. $64.50; 7. 65°; 8. angle *UVW*

Page 75
Fluency Blast: 4, 49, 10, 18, 9, 6; **Day 1:** 1. >; 2,
65,370; 3. 4,495; 4. 196; 5. 3 1/3; **Day 2:** 1. 1,138,
1,148, 1,158, 1,168; 2. 17/90 more; **Day 3:** 1–2. Check
students' work. 3. 75°; **Day 4:** 1. A; 2. obtuse;
3. Check students' work. equilateral

Page 76
1. 1,033, 1,053, 1,073, 1,093; 2. >; 3. 135 marbles;
4. obtuse; 5. Check students' work. 6. 1 1/3 gal.;
7. 105°; 8. right, isosceles

Page 77
Fluency Blast: 2, 30, 9, 35, 12, 64; **Day 1:** 1. 234,800;
2. five hundred sixty thousand six hundred
fifty-four; 3. 18; 4. Check students' work.
Day 2: 1. 5 2/3 yd.; 2. 2,000, 3,000, 4,000, 5,000;
Day 3: 1–4. Check students' work. **Day 4:** 1. C;
2. Check students' work, scalene; 3. $\overrightarrow{XY}$

Page 78
1. 30,000; 2. 7 1/2 ft.; 3. 91 stamps; 4. Check
students' work. 5. 45; 6. 738 boxes; 7. Check
students' work. 8. $\overline{DE}$

Page 79
Fluency Blast: 0.2, 0.9, 0.8, 0.5, 0.4, 0.3, 0.88, 0.52,
0.25, 0.55, 0.30, 0.14; **Day 1:** 1. 31,542; 2. 6 7/8;
3. 1,232, 173; 4. Check students' work.
Day 2: 1. 40 bags, 26 bags; 2. 81 daisies;
3. 3 13/15 mi.; **Day 3:** 1. 45°; 2. 75°; 3. 88°; **Day 4:** 1.
C; 2. $\overleftrightarrow{WX}$

Page 80
1. Check students' work. 2. 2,088 bottles of water;
3. 2,049, 199; 4. 27,773; 5. 1 37/63; 6. 18,101; 7. 65°;
8. $\overleftrightarrow{CD}$

Answer Key

Page 81

Fluency Blast: 5/10, 9/10, 7/10, 6/10, 8/10, 4/10, 62/100, 58/100, 22/100, 36/100, 25/100, 78/100; **Day 1:** 1. 4 1/2; 2. <; 3. 89,980; 4. Check students' work. **Day 2:** 1. oval; 2. 153 toothbrushes; 3. 18 tourists; **Day 3:** 1. 119°; 2. 138°; 3. 115°; **Day 4:** 1. scalene triangle; 2. $\overline{JK}$; 3. Check students' work.

Page 82

1. 14; 2. 15,000; 3. <; 4. 59; 5. 0.07; 6. 50; 7. 22°; 8. $\overrightarrow{LM}$

Page 83

Fluency Blast: 3/4, 1/8, 4/7, 3/4, 1/2, 3/8, 1/4, 1/2, 1/4, 2/3, 1/5, 1/5; **Day 1:** 1. 7/11; 2. 11,751; 3. 11,201; 4. >; 5. 0.45; **Day 2:** 1. 2/10 or 1/5 of the sandwich; 2. 78 stickers; 3. 327 gems; **Day 3:** 1. 30°; 2. 142°; 3. Check students' work. **Day 4:** Answers will vary but may include: 1. A, B, C, D; 2. $\overrightarrow{AB}$, $\overrightarrow{DE}$; 3. $\overleftrightarrow{AB}$, $\overleftrightarrow{CG}$; 4. $\overrightarrow{CB}$, $\overrightarrow{FE}$, $\overrightarrow{FG}$.

Page 84

1. >; 2. 44,441; 3. 3 1/3; 4. 1/2; 5. 1 7/8 cups; 6. 27 marshmallows with 8 left over; 7–8. Check students' work.

Page 85

Fluency Blast: 1/4, 1/3, 1/2, 1/3, 1/5, 1/2, 1/4, 2/3, 3/4, 1/2, 1/2, 2/3; **Day 1:** 1. 17/24; 2. 3/4; 3. 57; 4. 0.6; 5. 140,000; **Day 2:** 1. 1/8 gal.; 2. 135, 147, 159, 168; **Day 3:** 1. 142°; 2. 63°; 3. Check students' work. **Day 4:** Answers will vary but may include: 1. A, B, E; 2. $\overleftrightarrow{AE}$, $\overleftrightarrow{DB}$; 3. $\overline{BA}$, $\overline{BD}$, $\overline{BC}$, $\overline{BE}$; 4. $\overrightarrow{BA}$, $\overrightarrow{BD}$, $\overrightarrow{BC}$, $\overrightarrow{BE}$

Page 86

1. 2 2/3; 2. 0.33; 3. 63; 4. 2 19/36; 5. $3.35; 6. 33 years old; 7. 49°; 8. Check students' work.

Page 87

Fluency Blast: 1/3, 1/4, 1/6, 1/3, 1/3, 1/5, 1/4, 1/3, 1/3, 5/7, 1/4, 4/5; **Day 1:** 1. 6 1/8; 2. 1 1/2; 3. 0.65; 4. >; 5. 6; **Day 2:** 1. $1,427; 2. 21 marbles; 3. 4 gal.; **Day 3:** 1. 63°; 2. 38°; 3. 158°; **Day 4:** 1. yes; 2. yes; 3. yes; 4. no, Check students' work.

Page 88

1. $1,940; 2. 2 23/24; 3. 19/60; 4. 5/6 of the pizzas; 5. 709; 6. $4,500; 7. 50°; 8. yes, Check students' work.

CD-104974 • © Carson-Dellosa

Notes

Notes

CD-104974 • © Carson-Dellosa